blue
rider
press

the princess diarist

also by carrie fisher

Shockaholic

Wishful Drinking

The Best Awful: A Novel

Delusions of Grandma

Surrender the Pink

Postcards from the Edge

the princess diarist

carrie fisher

BLUE RIDER PRESS
New York

blue
rider
press

An imprint of Penguin Random House LLC
375 Hudson Street
New York, New York 10014

ISBN 9780399173592

Printed in the United States of America
1 3 5 7 9 10 8 6 4 2

BOOK DESIGN BY NICOLE LAROCHE

Penguin is committed to publishing works of quality and integrity. In that spirit, we are proud to offer this book to our readers; however, the story, the experiences, and the words are the author's alone.

FOR

George Lucas

Harrison Ford

Mark Hamill

Irvin Kershner

J. J. Abrams

Rian Johnson

the princess diarist

it was 1976 . . .

Charlie's Angels, *Laverne & Shirley*, and *Family Feud* premiered on TV.

Steve Wozniak and Steve Jobs founded the Apple computer company in a garage.

The Food and Drug Administration banned Red Dye No. 2 after it was found to cause tumors in the bladders of dogs.

Howard Hughes died at age seventy of kidney failure in a private jet en route to a Houston hospital. He was worth more than $2 billion and weighed 90 pounds.

Anne Rice's debut novel, *Interview with the Vampire*, was published.

Israel rescued 102 Air France passengers who were being held hostage at the Entebbe Airport in Uganda.

The Queen sent the first royal e-mail, London was bombed by the IRA and the Sex Pistols, and Queen's "Bohemian Rhapsody" went gold.

Andy Williams's ex-wife Claudine Longet accidentally, she claimed, shot her skier lover, Spider Sabich, to death.

A Pennsylvania congressman won renomination for a 12th term despite having been dead for two weeks.

Caitlyn Jenner, still Bruce then, won the gold medal in the Olympic decathlon, and the title "World's Greatest Athlete."

So many things were happening.

The first Ebola outbreak occurred in Africa, there was a panic over swine flu, and in a contaminated Philadelphia hotel, Legionnaires' disease killed twenty-nine people.

A military coup deposed Argentina's president Isabel Perón.

Sal Mineo was stabbed to death, and Agatha Christie and André Malraux died, though not together.

Saul Bellow won the Pulitzer Prize for *Humboldt's Gift* and the Nobel Prize for Literature for his body of work.

Son of Sam killed his first victim.

Riots in Soweto marked the beginning of the end of apartheid in South Africa.

The rock band that would become U2 was formed.

The United States Tennis Association barred transsexual Renée Richards from playing in the U.S. Open.

Network gave us Howard Beale's iconic rant, "I'm as mad as hell and I'm not going to take this anymore," and Paul Simon won the Grammy Award for Album of the Year for *Still Crazy After All These Years.*

Jimmy Carter beat Gerald Ford, even after saying in a *Playboy* interview that he lusted after women in his heart.

Ryan Reynolds and Benedict Cumberbatch were born, as were Colin Farrell, Rashida Jones, Alicia Silverstone, Rick Ross, Anna Faris, Peyton Manning, Audrey Tautou, Ja Rule, and Reese Witherspoon.

George Harrison was found guilty of plagiarizing "He's So Fine" for "My Sweet Lord."

Buffalo Bills running back O. J. Simpson had the best game of his career, rushing a then record 273 yards and scoring two touchdowns against the Detroit Lions.

Mao Tse-tung died.

The Supreme Court reinstated the death penalty, ruling that this punishment was not particularly cruel or unusual.

The Band played its farewell concert in San Francisco.

Elizabeth Taylor and Richard Burton separated after four months of marriage, which had been preceded by sixteen months of divorce.

America celebrated its bicentennial.

I think you get the picture. It was a year that, like all years, a lot of things happened in. People were on TV or in movies, they wrote songs that were liked more than other songs, while other people excelled at sports, and, as always, a lot of accomplished and famous people died. But through it all, one big thing that was beginning to happen—and that still, lo these many decades later, hasn't stopped happening—is *Star Wars*.

We were filming *Star Wars* in London in 1976, and none of us in the cast had any idea how significantly our lives would be altered when the movie premiered the following year.

Cut to: 2013. Much the same kinds of things were happening, only faster and more intensely. And George Lucas announced that the *Star Wars* franchise was starting up again, and that the original cast would be in it.

I was surprised. As surprised as you can be and still be so far over forty. I mean, I thought they might make more *Star Wars* movies—not that I thought about it all that much—but I doubted that I would find myself in them. And now it looked like I would! Hallelujah!

Not because I liked appearing up on a screen. I didn't like it when I was the age one *could* like it, but now they had 3-D and high-def and such, so that all your wrinkles and withered puffiness need their own agents, so if I didn't like it then, I'd never like it now, and going forward to eventually. The bummer was that I wouldn't be able to watch the new sequel. Not with me in it. But to hell with that! Someone could tell me about it!

If I was going to do the new *Star Wars*, they'd have to pay me *something*, even though the cloud of doubt could easily and gradually be cast over that potential fact based on some of the history of the *Star Wars* company. (No merchandising! But maybe I'd get some this time!)

And they'd have us all over the barrel of our wanting to be in it. And they could just as easily write any of us out. Well, maybe not easily, but they could write us out if we wrangled too long over what we wanted to be paid. And by "we," in this case, I mean "I."

And as much as I may have joked about *Star Wars* over the years, *I liked that I was in those films*. Particularly as the only girl in an all-boy fantasy. They were fun to make. It was an anecdote of unimaginable standing.

I *liked* being Princess Leia. Or Princess Leia's being me. Over time I thought that we'd melded into one. I don't think you could think of Leia without my lurking in that thought somewhere. And I'm not talking about masturbation. So Princess Leia are us.

Bottom line, I was going to be able to pay some if not all of my overhead! Maybe not now, but soon. Sure, if it wasn't very soon I'd be paying bills from an apartment, but at least I'd be able to buy stuff I didn't need again. Stuff I didn't need and in such unnecessary quantities! I'd maybe even have a charge at Barneys again soon! Life was good! Public life, that is... swimming pools, movie stars...

And this, ladies and gentlemoons, is how my whole new *Star Wars* adventure began! Like an acid flashback, only intergalactic, in the moment, and essentially real!

Who do I think I would've been if I hadn't been Princess Leia? Am I Princess Leia, or is she me? Split the difference and you'd be closer to the truth. *Star Wars* was and is my job. It can't fire me and I'll never be able to quit, and why would I want to? (That's both a rhetorical and a real question.)

Today, while going through some boxes containing some old writing of mine, I found the diaries I kept while filming the first *Star Wars* movie forty years ago. Stay tuned.

life before leia

Two years before *Star Wars* I'd been in a film called *Shampoo*, starring and produced by Warren Beatty and directed by Hal Ashby. I played the part of Lee Grant's angry promiscuous daughter, who ends up having sex with her mother's lover/hairdresser—the starring role played, of course, by Warren. It was he, along with the screenwriter Robert Towne, who hired me for the pissed-off-daughter role.

At the time, the last thing I thought I wanted to do was go into show business, a fickle occupation that doled out a sense of uneasiness and humiliation like tepid snacks at movie screenings. This uneasiness was nurtured by the almost invisible diminishment over time of one's popularity. First you're in movies—a few small parts in popular films.

Then, if it happens, the thing all actors are waiting for—stardom. You're a years-in-the-making overnight success.

I had missed the early giddy portion of my parents' rise to success. I arrived on the scene when my mother, Debbie Reynolds, was still making good, big-budget films at MGM. But as I grew up and my consciousness all too slowly snapped into focus, I noticed that the films were not what they had originally been. Her contract expired when she was in her late thirties. I recall her last MGM Studios film at forty was of the horror variety, entitled *What's the Matter with Helen?* This was no *Singin' in the Rain*, and her costar Shelley Winters somewhat thoughtlessly killed her at the film's close.

Soon after this, my mother began doing nightclub work in Las Vegas at the now-defunct Desert Inn. Coincidentally, I also began doing nightclub work, singing "I Got Love" and "Bridge over Troubled Water" in her show. It was a huge step up for me from high school. My younger brother, Todd, accompanied me on guitar, and my mother's backup singers danced and sang behind me (something that, at occasional odd moments throughout my life, I've wished that they continued to do).

My mother then took a modified version of this show to theaters and fairs across America. After that she did a Broadway musical. I was then one of the backup singers behind her, where backup singers tend to lurk. She then continued to do her nightclub act for the next forty years—with forays into television shows and films (most notably in Albert Brooks's *Mother*).

My father, Eddie Fisher, played in nightclubs until he was no longer asked to, and when he wasn't asked to it was in part because as a crooner he was no longer relevant, and in part because he was more interested in sex and drugs than anything else. Shooting speed for thirteen years can really put a crimp in whatever career you might otherwise be attempting to sustain—ask around.

Periodically, he would manage to secure a book deal or—well, actually, that's it. No one could take the risk of hiring him to sing; he could easily be a no-show, and his vocal range was severely limited by his debauched lifestyle. Also, people found it difficult to forgive him for leaving my mother for Elizabeth Taylor all those years ago, causing him to be viewed for his remaining years as "America's Cad."

One day when I was about twelve I was sitting on my grandmother's lap—not a good idea at any age, given that Maxine Reynolds was, to say the least, not a cuddly woman—when she suddenly asked my mother, "Hey, did you ever get those tickets to *Annie* that I asked you for?"

She regarded my mother with suspicious eyes. (My grandmother had three looks: glaring suspiciously, glaring hostilely, and glaring with disappointment—active disappointment, lively disappointment, condescending disappointment.)

"I'm sorry, Mama," my mother responded. "Is there another show you want to see? *Annie* seems to be sold out for the whole month. I've tried everywhere."

My grandmother pursed her lips, giving the appearance of someone who smelled something bad. Then she pushed air out of her nose and pronounced a very disappointed "Hmmmmmm."

"It used to mean something in this town to be Debbie Reynolds," she said. "Now she can't even get a few measly show tickets." I involuntarily squeezed my grandmother, as if to do so would push all future demeaning remarks out of her stocky little body. It was episodes like this that made me decide: I never wanted to be in show business.

So why did I agree to visit the set of *Shampoo* knowing that there might be a role in the film that I was right for? Go figure. Maybe I wanted to see what it felt like to be wanted by Warren Beatty in any capacity at all. At any rate, at seventeen I didn't see it as a career choice. Or perhaps I was kidding myself—Lord knows it wouldn't be the last time in my life I would do that. Kidding yourself doesn't require that you have a sense of humor. But a sense of humor comes in handy for almost everything else. Especially the darker things, which this did not fall anywhere under the heading of.

I got the role of Lorna in *Shampoo*. Lorna, the daughter of Jack Warden and Lee Grant. I basically had one scene and that scene was with Warren, who played my mother's, and everyone else in the film's, hairdresser and lover. My character doesn't like her mother and has never had her hair done (i.e., slept with her hairdresser).

Was Lorna's not getting her hair done a way of rebelling against her mother? Possibly. Was propositioning her mother's hairdresser a way of screwing with her hated mother? Absolutely. Would Lorna have been sorry if her father found out? Probably. Or not. You pick.

In the film, I am discovered on the tennis court wearing a tennis outfit, holding a racquet, and standing next to a tennis pro who is hitting balls as I watch Warren arrive. I inform him that my mother is not at home and take him to the kitchen, where I ask him if he's making it with my mother and if he wants anything to eat. I tell him I've never been to a hairdresser, that I'm nothing like my mother, and ask him if he wants to fuck. The scene ends with my proposition and we then find me in the bedroom, postcoitally reapplying my headscarf.

Why did I wear a headscarf, you most likely failed to wonder? Because I, Carrie, had short hair—the kind you get from going to a hairdresser—so I had to wear a wig to show that a visit to a hairdresser was not something that would ever be found on my schedule. I wore the scarf because the wig looked less like a wig that way. The other big question you're probably not asking yourself is, did I wear a bra under my tennis outfit (and if I didn't, why didn't I)?

Simple. Warren, the star, cowriter, and producer of *Shampoo,* was asked by the costume department if he wanted me to wear a bra under my tennis clothes or not. Warren squinted in the general direction of my breasts.

"Is she wearing one now?"

I stood there as if my breasts and I were somewhere else.

"Yes," responded Aggie, the costume designer.

Warren pursed his lips thoughtfully. "Let's see it without."

I followed Aggie to my hamster-cage trailer and removed my bra. Whereupon I was returned to Warren's scrutiny forthwith. Once again he squinted at my chest impassively.

"And this is without?" he asked.

"Yes," Aggie groaned.

"Let's go without," he pronounced, directed, charged, commanded.

My breasts and I followed Aggie back to my dressing zone and the subject was closed. My braless *Shampoo* breasts can be ogled on YouTube (or LubeTube), as can my no-underwear-in-space look in the first *Star Wars* and the metal bikini (or Jabba Killer) in the third (now confusingly known as *Episodes IV* and *VI*).

My two scenes in *Shampoo* took only a few days to shoot, and when they were done I went back to living at home with my mother and younger brother, Todd, hoping that I wouldn't be living there for too much longer, as any amount of time was way too long for the now-too-hip-for-words me.

I had never had an audition like the one I had with Terrence Malick, the director of *Days of Heaven*. I recall sitting with him for over an hour and talking. Not just me talking, thank God—though I do think the emphasis was on getting to know me and what I was like. After all, *I* hadn't called *him* into a room to meet about a movie *I* was making.

I remember telling him far too much about myself, a habit that would only increase as I aged. But as a teenager I didn't yet have that big a repertoire of anecdotes. One of my best up to that time had to do with the comic Rip Taylor—he and my mom did a show together in Vegas—and his gay secretary, Lynn.

I had a crush on Lynn. He was good-looking, wore an ascot, and was really dainty, like if you breathed on him he would fall over like a feather in the wind. Lynn used to call me his love apple, and we would make out on the crew's bus.

If I'd been in high school instead of doing shows with my mother, I'd have had appropriate venues for my adolescent feelings to emerge. I would have lived a life as a teenager, but since I wasn't living that life, I kept having crushes on gay men.

Besides Lynn, there was also Albert, who was a dancer in the Broadway show *Irene* with Debbie. He was attractive and gay (although in my uninformed opinion you wouldn't pick him out as gay), and we used to make out in the dressing rooms. My mom knew about this, so what the fuck was that about? I was only fifteen, and I was jailbait, and my mom said, "If you want to have sex with Albert, I'll watch if you like so I can give instructions."

To be fair, my mom was really distracted then—her whole life was falling apart, so she was trying to anchor it by providing some admittedly and/or eccentric motherly love.

There aren't many perfect moments to air out a story like that, so I'm fairly certain Terry Malick heard about Lynn and Albert and my mom. He seemed the type of person who was interested in hearing just about any weird story you had that left you feeling frightened and alone. He did a lot of improvisation in his films, so these interviews may have been his way of determining if his actors were comfortable in their own skin. (I'm someone who's *very* comfortable in my own skin. I just wish there wasn't so much room at times for that comfort.)

We had several such meetings together before Malick had me read with John Travolta. John was famous then from his television sitcom *Welcome Back, Kotter*. It seemed to be understood that John had the "inside track" for the lead role in *Days of Heaven*, and, in the few times we read together, John and I had great chemistry. Like two beakers containing flammable liquid, we bubbled along together comfortably. If John starred in *Days of Heaven*, would I star alongside him? Things were looking good for me.

And then, for some reason, John couldn't do the film. So John was out and Richard Gere was in. I read with Richard Gere. Let's just say our beakers didn't bubble with compatibility. So now I was out and Brooke Adams was in. My potential career as a serious-ish actress was—for now anyway—at an end. It would take more than a cameo in *The Blues Brothers* to get people to stop thinking of me as Princess Leia.

Days of Heaven was a wonderful film and perhaps would've de-Leia'd me a little, but my very, very light cross to bear would always be that I would be known as Princess Leia and not as That Girl Who Was So Good in One of Terry Malick's Early Masterpieces.

I auditioned for other films (*Grease* and *The Fortune*)

and then I applied to two drama schools in England. The Royal Academy of Dramatic Art would have none of me, but the Central School of Speech and Drama—whose notable alumni included Laurence Olivier, Harold Pinter, and the Redgrave sisters—said yes.

This was what I'd been selfishly waiting for: the chance to stop living at home with—or even in the *same country* with—my newly divorced and newly broke-ish mother. As a bonus, I got real acting experience, which I'd never had, partly because I still wasn't so sure that I wanted to be an actress. But maybe it was something I could do without a high school diploma or accredited skills of any kind whatsoever—a job that would pay me enough of a wage to let me go out into the world and start what I would laughingly come to call my own actual life.

When I began attending Central I was seventeen, and the youngest student there. It was the first time I actually lived on my own. I was finally away from my mother (whom I'd happily live off of but not with), in an apartment I was subletting from a friend, where no one could be disappointed in me—and if someone oddly should be, I didn't care, because they weren't related to me.

upside down and unconscious with yellow eyes

George Lucas held his auditions for *Star Wars* in an office on a lot in Hollywood. It was in one of those faux-Spanish cream-colored buildings from the thirties with dark orange-tiled roofs and black-iron-grated windows, lined with sidewalks in turn lined with trees—pine trees, I think they were, the sort that shed their needles generously onto the street below—and interrupted by parched patches of once-green lawns.

Everything was a little worse for the wear, but good things would happen in these buildings. Lives would be led, businesses would prosper, and men would attend meetings—hopeful meetings, meetings where big plans were made and ideas were proposed. But of all the meetings that had ever been held in that particular office, none of them could compare in world impact with the casting calls for the *Star Wars* movie.

A plaque could be placed on the outside of this building that states, "On this spot the *Star Wars* films conducted their casting sessions. In this building the actors and actresses entered and exited until only three remained. These three were the actors who ultimately played the lead parts of Han, Luke, and Leia."

I've told the story of getting cast as Princess Leia many times before—in interviews, on horseback, and in cardiac units—so if you've previously heard this story before, I apologize for requiring some of your coveted store of patience. I know how closely most of us tend to hold on to whatever cache of patience we've managed to amass over a lifetime and I appreciate your squandering some of your cherished stash here.

George gave me the impression of being smaller than he was because he spoke so infrequently. I first encountered his all-but-silent presence at these auditions—the first of which he held with the director Brian De Palma. Brian was casting his horror film *Carrie*, and they both required an actress between the age of eighteen and twenty-two. I was the right age at the right time, so I read for both George and Brian.

George had directed two other feature films up till then, *THX 1138*, starring Robert Duvall, and *American Graffiti*, starring Ron Howard and Cindy Williams. The roles I met with the two directors for that first day were Princess Leia in *Star Wars* and Carrie in *Carrie*. I thought that last role would be a funny casting coup if I got it: Carrie *as* Carrie *in Carrie*. I doubt that that was why I never made it to the next level with *Carrie*—but it didn't help as far as I was concerned that there would have to be a goofy film poster advertising a serious horror film.

I sat down before the two directors behind their respective desks. Mr. Lucas was all but mute. He nodded when I entered the room, and Mr. De Palma took over from there. He was a big man, and not merely because he spoke more—or spoke, period. Brian sat on the left and George on the right, both bearded. As if you had two choices in director sizes. Only I didn't have the choice—they did.

Brian cleared his bigger throat of bigger things and said, "So I see here you've been in the film *Shampoo*?"

I knew this, so I simply nodded, my face in a tight white-toothed smile. Maybe they would ask me something requiring more than a nod.

"Did you enjoy working with Warren?"

"Yes, I did!" That was easy! I had enjoyed working with him, but Brian's look told me that wasn't enough of an answer. "He was . . ."

What was he? They needed to know! "He helped me work . . . a lot. I mean, he and the other screenwriter . . . they worked with me." Oh my God, this wasn't going well.

Mr. De Palma waited for more, and when more wasn't forthcoming, he attempted to help me. "How did they work with you?"

Oh, that's what they wanted to know! "They had me do the scene over and over, and with food. There was eating in the scene. I had to offer Warren a baked apple and then I ask him if he's making it with my mother—sleeping with her—you know."

George almost smiled; Brian actually did. "Yes, I know what 'making it' means."

I flushed. I considered stopping this interview then and there. But I soldiered on.

"No, no, that's the dialogue. 'Are you making it with my mother?' I asked him that because I hate my mother. Not in real life, I hate my mother in the movie, partly because she is sleeping with Warren—who's the hairdresser. Lee Grant played my mom, but I didn't really have any scenes with her, which is too bad because she's a great actress. And Warren is a great actor and he also wrote the movie, with Robert Towne, which is why they both worked with me. With food. It sounded a lot more natural when you talk with food in your mouth. Not that you do that in your movies. Maybe in the scary movie, but I don't know the food situation in space." The meeting seemed to be going better.

"What have you done since *Shampoo*?" George asked.

I repressed the urge to say I had written three symphonies and learned how to perform dental surgery on monkeys, and instead told the truth.

"I went to school in England. Drama school. I went to the Central School of Speech and Drama." I was breathless with information. "I mean I didn't just go, I'm still going. I'm home on Christmas vacation."

I stopped abruptly to breathe. Brian was nodding, his eyebrows headed off to his hair in something like surprise. He asked me politely about my experience at school, and I responded politely as George watched impassively. (I would come to discover that George's expression wasn't indifferent or anything like it. It was shy and discerning, among many other things, including intelligent, studious, and—and a word like "darling." Only not that word, because it's too young and androgynous, and besides which, and most important, George would hate it.)

"What do you plan on doing if you get one of these jobs you're meeting on?" continued Brian.

"I mean, it really would depend on the part, but . . . I guess I'd leave. I mean I know I would. Because I mean—"

"I know what you mean," Brian interrupted. The meeting continued but I was no longer fully present—utterly convinced that I'd screwed up by revealing myself to be so disloyal. Leave my school right in the middle for the first job that came along?

Soon after, we were done. I shook each man's hand as I moved to the door, leading off to the gallows of obscurity. George's hand was firm and cool.

I returned to the outer office knowing full well that I would be going back to school. "Miss Fisher," a casting assistant said. I froze, or would have, if we weren't in sunny Los Angeles. "Here are your sides. Two doors down. You'll read on video." My heart pounded everywhere a pulse can get to.

The scene from *Carrie* involved the mother (who would be memorably played by Piper Laurie). A dark scene, where the people are not okay. But the scene in *Star Wars*—there were no mothers there! There was authority and confidence and command in the weird language that was used. Was I like this? Hopefully George would think so, and I could pretend I thought so, too. I could pretend I was a princess whose life went from chaos to crisis without looking down between chaoses to find, to her relief, that her dress wasn't torn.

I have no recollection now of how I felt reading the two scenes. I can only assume I beat myself up loud and long. Did they like me? Did they think I was fat? Did they think I looked like a bowl of oatmeal with features? Four little dark dots in one big flat pale face ("Me pale face—you Tonto"). Did they think I looked pretty enough? Was I likable enough for me to relax at all? Not on your life. Because (a) there was no relaxing anywhere in my general area, and (b) there was no relaxing anywhere in show business.

But George must have thought I did well enough to have me back. They sent me the *Star Wars* script so I could practice it before the last reading. I remember opening the manila envelope it came in very carefully, one edge at a time, before removing its unknown cargo. It didn't look any different from other scripts—cardboard-like paper on each end, protecting the ordinary paper within—covered in antlike scratches of letters. I don't know why, but I wanted to read this screenplay out loud.

Enter Miguel Ferrer. Miguel wasn't certain that he wanted to be an actor yet—like me. But we were both intrigued enough that we continued exploring. Like me, he came from a show business background. His father was the actor José Ferrer and his mother the singer/actress Rosemary Clooney. We were friends, and I called him up and asked him to read this script with me. He arrived at my mother's newer, much smaller house—since her dramatically reduced financial circumstances due to a second failed marriage—and we went to my bedroom on the second floor.

Like every young man wanting to be an actor in Hollywood then, he had also read for the film, so both of us were dimly aware what we were in store for. We sat on my bed and began to read. From the first page—STAR WARS: A SPACE FANTASY—the images and characters jumped off the pages. Not only into our minds, but into the chairs and other furniture that surrounded us. I'm exaggerating (a little) but it could have jumped onto the furniture, eaten all of it, and drank the blood of an Englishman—because it was as epic as any fee-fi-fo-fum rhyme you ever heard.

The images of space opened around us, planets and stars floated by. The character I was reading for, Leia, was kidnapped by the evil Darth Vader—kidnapped and hung upside down when the smuggler pilot Han Solo (who Miguel was reading for) and his giant monkey creature copilot Chewbacca rescued me. I had been (in the script) upside down and unconscious with yellow eyes. I'll never forget that image. Whoever got the part of the princess named Leia would get to do this. I would potentially get to do this! Maybe—if I was lucky—I would be rescued by Han and Chewbacca (Chewie!) from the caverns underneath wherever they'd tortured me, and Chewie would carry me, slung over his shoulder through thigh deep water as we made it out of (interplanetary) harm's way.

Unfortunately, none of this imagery was ever realized due to a combination of cost and the fact that Peter Mayhew—who they hired to play Chewie—couldn't do the stunt due to his extreme height of over 7 feet. He had a condition that left him unable to stand up quickly and remain stable; it was impossible for him to lift up weight of any kind. And my weight, as everyone at Lucasland can recall, was, and remains, of the "any kind" variety.

But I can safely say that any girl cast in the part of the feisty Princess Leia would've been of the any kind size—because once Peter was cast, the lifting and being carried through those thigh-high drenched caverns was out. But I also recall hearing that the water-engulfed caverns were quite an expensive set to build, and this was a low-budget film, so they were out for that reason—leaving only Leia's unconsciousness and those yellow eyes. Most of us know how inexpensive unconsciousness is or was to achieve, so that wouldn't have been a budget problem—just inappropriate. But by the time you lose Peter's inability to carry any feisty princess and consider the cost-ineffective underground water caverns—it doesn't matter how beautifully you can portray insensibility—it ain't happening anyway.

The Force was put in me (in a non-invasive way) by the script that day with Miguel, and it has remained in me ever since. I ended up reading for the film with a new actor, an actor I'd never seen before, but then he had never seen me, either. I'll bet since that reading with me he's rued the day—if he can get his strong hands on a rue that is—and if anyone could get their hands on a rue or a Woo it was Harrison Ford. We read together in a room in that same building I'd met George and Brian De Palma in. I was so nervous about the reading I don't remember much about Harrison, and given how nervous Harrison would come to make me, that was plenty frightened indeed.

The following week, my agent, a man who'd been my mother's agent, Wilt Melnick, and was now mine, called me.

"Carrie?" he asked.

I knew my name. So I let him know I knew it. "Yeah," I said in a voice very like mine. Mine but hollow, mine but it didn't matter because my stomach had swung into action.

"They called," he said.

Great, 'cause that was really all I wanted to know. If they called, that they called, not what they said—that didn't matter.

"They want you," he continued.

There was a silence.

"They do? I mean they did?"

He laughed, then I laughed and dropped the phone and ran out into the front yard and into the street. It was raining. It didn't rain in L.A. It was raining in L.A. and I was Princess Leia. I had never been Princess Leia before and now I would be her forever. I would never not be Princess Leia. I had no idea how profoundly true that was and how long forever was.

They would pay me nothing and fly me economy—a fact that would haunt my mother for months—but I was Leia and that was all that truly mattered. I'm Leia—I can live in a tree, but you can't take that away from me.

I never dreamt there actually might be a day when I maybe hoped that you could.

the buns of navarone

The movie was being shot in England, so I could drop out of school but wouldn't have to leave the scene of the crime. My friend Riggs let me use his flat in Kensington, behind Barkers department store, and that's where I stayed for the three-month duration of the film.

I remember arriving on the set that first day, attempting to seem as benignly unobtrusive as I possibly could. I showed up at the studio in Borehamwood—about forty-five minutes outside of London—where they fitted me for wardrobe and did hair and makeup tests. (The crew was mostly men. That's how it was and that's pretty much how it still is. It's a man's world and show business is a man's meal, with women generously sprinkled through it like overqualified spice.)

The hairstyle that was chosen would impact how everyone—every filmgoing human—would envision me for the rest of my life. (And probably even beyond—it's hard to imagine any TV obituary not using a photo of that cute little round-faced girl with goofy buns on either side of her inexperienced head.) My life had started, all right. Here I was crossing its threshold in a long white virginal robe with the hair of a seventeenth-century Dutch school matron.

I was awarded the part in *Star Wars* with the dispiriting caveat that I lose ten pounds, so for me the experience was less like, "*All right! I got a job!*" and more like, "I got a job and I hurt my ankle." The minus 10 percent was an agent's fee, in flesh.

So I went to a fat farm. In Texas. Weren't there any fat farms around Los Angeles? The only answers I can think of are (1) no, because everyone in Los Angeles was already thin, and (2) no, because this was 1976, years before the whole exercising, body-obsessed, fat-farm thing would take hold. The only exercise guru then was Richard Simmons—a flamboyant fuzzy-haired creature who vaguely resembled a gay Bozo the Clown, unless that's redundant, which I, thank God, have no way of knowing, having no, thank God, direct experience with Bozo the Clown.

My mother recommended the Green Door in Texas, but it was probably called the Golden Door or something else because the only Green Door that anyone had heard of was a porn film, *Behind the Green Door*, which was known for making its star, Marilyn Chambers, if not a household name then a whorehouse-hold name. (I had seen it at fifteen, not having heard the phrase "blow job" before.)

At the Texas fat farm, I met Ann Landers (aka Eppie Lederer), a famous advice columnist, and Lady Bird Johnson, who both took me under their (overweight) wings, which was an uncomfortable place to be. Lady Bird, when I told her the title of *Star Wars*, thought I'd said *Car Wash*, and Ann/Eppie gave me a lot of unsolicited advice over a less-than-filling dinner of a burnt-looking partridge that seemed to have been singed and then torched. It was still more than enough; with a heavy heart and heavier face, I left a week later.

When we started filming, I tried to keep myself well under the radar so that the powers that be wouldn't notice that I hadn't lost the weight they'd asked me to. I only weighed 110 pounds to begin with, but I carried about half of them in my face. I think they may have put those buns on me so they might function as bookends, keeping my face right where it was, between my ears and no bigger.

There I would stay, cheeks in check—my face as round as I was short, but no rounder.

We usually finished shooting around six thirty p.m., Monday through Friday. The unluckiest members of the cast—a group that definitely included me—were summoned to the set at around five a.m. I rose before dawn; was picked up at my flat in Kensington by my cheerful driver, Colin; and was spirited through the largely still sleeping London to the rosy dawn hem of its outskirts, arriving some forty-five minutes later at the less-than-stern guardrail of Borehamwood Elstree Studios.

Why was I asked to arrive at this ungodly hour? What monstrous chain of command had selected me apart from many others more deserving, more endowed with tresses thick and wavy tumbling toward their waiting waists?

Perhaps by now the sci-fi aficionados have guessed it. Yes, that god-awfully laughable Leia hairstyle! There were two hairpieces that were practically bolted to each side of my head. First one, then the other, these long brown tresses that, once latched on grimly, were twisted into some oversized-cinnamon-bun shape, which then—with a deftness that never ceased to amaze me—the hairdresser would very slowly and deliberately wind into the now-famous buns of Navarone.

Pat McDermott was the hairdresser assigned to supply me with the hairstyle that I would wear in the movie. Having only worn one hairstyle in *Shampoo*, I couldn't see how this could be anything but a straightforward task. Apply a wig, brush some hair, affix some hairpins—voilà, hairstyle. What could be simpler? Well, this straightforward task turned out to be a little more than that when you considered Leia's look would be something worn by children, transvestites, and couples involved in what might be considered a sex fantasy immortalized on the show *Friends*. There might have been more responsibility involved than first met the eye. Of course, there was no way to know this initially. So Pat attempted to deliver what was requested of her, an unusual hairstyle to be worn by a nineteen-year-old girl playing a princess.

Pat was from Ireland and spoke with a lovely Irish brogue—causing (or enabling, depending on the morning) her to refer to a movie as a "fill-um." She also called me "My lovely" or "My dearest girl": "Isn't this quite an amazing fill-um, my dearest girl" or "Who is this but my darlin' girl and that crazy hairstyle I put on her each and every day for the new fill-um they're makin'." I doubt she ever said the latter sentence for me, but she could have, and no one would be any the wiser.

Having arrived oh so early in the a.m., I would invariably fall asleep in the makeup chair, a plain girl with damp scraggly hair—falling just past the shoulder of whatever unprepossessing T-shirt I'd worn that day—and would miraculously awaken two hours later transformed from "Who the hell is she?" into the magnificently mighty mouthful herself, Princess Leia Organa, formerly of Alderaan and presently of anywhere and everywhere she damn well pleased.

I had endless issues with my appearance in *Star Wars*. Real ones—not ones you bring up so people think you're humble because you secretly find yourself adorable. What I saw in the mirror is not apparently what many teenage boys saw. If I'd known about all the masturbating I would generate—well, that would've been extraordinarily weird from many angles and I'm glad it didn't come up, as it were. But when men—fifty-year-old-plus men down to . . . well, the age goes pretty low for statutory comfort—when men approach me to let me know that I was their first love, let's just say I have mixed feelings. Why did all these men find it so easy to be in love with me then and so complex to be in love with me now?

I had no idea how much time Pat and I would spend together. She was the first person I saw in the morning and the last person I saw at night. But it was the morning bit that was the most intimate. Because the hair took two hours to style, we spent inordinate amounts of time coming up with conversation. The horror is sitting with someone silently. It's the conversational low. Sure, you can turn on music and sit or stand there smiling vaguely, trying to pretend there's nowhere else you'd rather be, but...

The sketches of hairstyles that Pat had been given to use as a guideline were shown to me. I looked at her aghast, with much like the expression I used when shown the sketches of the metal bikini. The one I wore to kill Jabba (my favorite moment in my own personal film history), which I highly recommend your doing: find an equivalent of killing a giant space slug in your head and celebrate that. It works wonders when I'm plagued by dark images of my hairy earphones.

So Pat showed me a variety of exotic looks—from Russian princesses to Swedish maids. I looked at the images, slightly alarmed. There was no Lady Gaga to guide me.

"These are meant to be worn by me?"

Pat smiled sympathetically. "Not all of them. Just one. And I'm sure they won't want you to wear anything you don't like."

I regarded her doubtfully. Those sounded like famous last words.

"You worry too much," Pat laughed, smoothing my hair back.

So image by image, we went through hairstyles that would look best when accompanied by clogs, an apron, and puffy white sleeves. A hairstyle probably sported by an

Aztec Indian chief's daughter on her wedding day. Swirling braids, flowing tresses, and towering wigs. I would sit miserably in front of a mirror and watch while hairstyles did to my face what fun house mirrors do to yours.

"This isn't a hairdo, it's a hair don't."

Pat would politely laugh at what I hoped would pass for wordplay and continue combing, pinning, spraying, teasing. And after each new hairstyle I would stand back at the mirror, gaze at the face, and struggle to make peace with my appearance. Was I round faced and adorable looking? Of course. I see that from this devious distance, but most of us look better at a distance.

Eventually, we arrived at the hairy-earphone configuration. "Well, what do you think of this one, darling? Be honest now. You're goin' to have to wear this hairstyle for a while." She had no idea exactly how long.

"It's okay," I managed. "I mean, I like it better than a lot of the others! I mean—no offense, but—"

"Oh, *pshaw*, darling—no offense taken. I'm just trying to give 'em what they want, though I'm not so sure they know precisely what that is."

"Can't it be something... simpler? I mean, why does the hair have to be... you know, so..."

"It's an outer-space fill-um, my lovely, we can't have you larkin' about wearin' what I think you call a ponytail [and here she yanked on my very own ponytail!] with a fringe, can we now?"

I was silent. I thought the ponytail, after all the braids and hairpieces, sounded... if not good, preferable.

"No, indeed, so let's you and me give the powers that be another little show, shall we?"

"Okay," I responded briskly, "let's get in there and kick some—" Pat looked at me and I smiled too broadly. "Fuck me twice and cover me with applesauce!"

We strolled onto the set, Pat looking clear-eyed and straight-backed with her silver hair and bright blue eyes, me looking as if all I needed was a dirndl, a goat, and clogs to be ready to take my place in *The Sound of Music*. We arrived at a small troop of traveling minstrels—no, I'm kidding. I wish we'd arrived at a small troop of traveling anything, instead of this group of three: the first assistant director David Tomblin, the producer Gary Kurtz, who might've been smiling under his usual fashion choice, a bearded straight face, and George.

"Well..." George practically said. Dave Tomblin spoke for the entire group when he repeated the same thing he'd said after at least six previous hair don'ts: "I think this one is quite..."

"...Flattering!" Gary finished.

"What do you think of it?" George asked me.

Now, remember, I hadn't lost the requisite ten pounds

and I thought any minute they'd notice and fire me before the film even started.

So, I replied, "I love it!"

It was also around then that I became uncontrollably enamored of a makeup enhancement that shames me even today: lip gloss. I had so much lip gloss on you might have slid off and broken your own lips if you tried to kiss me. I've never really understood what lip gloss is meant to enhance. Is that how much spit I leave on there when I lick my lips? Even if I was licking my lips in some come-hither way, that still wouldn't account for that slap of sticky shine. No tongue is that wet, or if it was, it would have to be the tongue of a buffalo—or my dog, Gary, who has a tongue the size of two city blocks, enabling him, if he so chooses, to lick his eyes. But if you got all of Gary's horrific long strands of spit slathered onto my—or some other unlucky lass's—lips, I doubt it would provide me with that come-hither look. It would give me more of a come-slather look.

Giving Leia that high-shine look would make Vader afraid he might slip on her lip gloss and fall on his breathing machine. And who wears that much lip gloss into battle? Me, or Leia, of course.

The late actress Joan Hackett was a much older friend who taught me many of the things my mother wisely or unwisely failed to, including a love for, and thus the philosophy behind, lip gloss. I've since seen Joan in a movie that takes place in the old West, and in it, she is wearing enough gloss to wax a car, and it works on her, mostly—it really does. But in the final analysis I've learned that space battle and lip gloss don't mix.

I don't remember much about things like the order we shot scenes in or who I got to know well first. Nor did anyone mention that one day I would be called upon to remember any of this long-ago experience. That one day soon, and then for all the days after that, information about *Star Wars* would be considered desirable in the extreme. That there would be an insatiable appetite for it, as if it were food in a worldwide famine.

Everywhere I looked, things were new. British crew: new. The way I was treated: new. The feeling that so many things were possible it was difficult to name them, or focus on them, for long: very new.

I read the dialogue and it was impossible. On my first day I had a scene with Peter Cushing, who played Governor Tarkin. This is the scene when I was supposed to say, "I thought I recognized your foul stench when I arrived on board." Who talks like that, except maybe a pirate in the seventeenth century? I looked at it and thought it should be said more like, "Hey, Governor Tarkin, I knew I'd see you here. When I got on board this ship I thought, My God! What is that smell? It's gotta be Governor Tarkin. Everyone knows that the guy smells like a wheel of cheese that someone found in their car after seven weeks!" So I did it like that, more sardonic than emotional. Fearless and like an actual human, but not serious. Ironic. Some chick from Long Island who's not scared of you or anyone you might know.

And this was when George gave me the only direction that I ever received from him other than his usual suggestion to make everything you're saying "faster" or "more intense." He took me aside and in a very solemn voice told me, "This is a very big deal for Leia. Huge. I mean, her planet is about to get blown up by these guys. And that means everything that she knows is gonna be gone forever. So you're very upset. *She* is very upset."

I listened carefully because I was the one with most of the earnest lines, and prior to this I didn't know whether I was going to have to deliver them earnestly. When you watch the movie, it turns out that the voice I used when I was upset was vaguely British, and my not-upset voice is less British.

• • •

Because I grimaced each time one of the blanks noisily exited my laser gun, I had to take shooting lessons from the policeman who prepared Robert De Niro for his terrifying, psychotic role in *Taxi Driver*. Actually, it wouldn't become a laser gun until post-production. Thus the expression "We'll fix it in post." (I wanted to be fixed in post, but this wouldn't become possible until the birth of collagen injections in Poland in the early eighties. As far as I know there have been no Polish jokes in conjunction with this important discovery. Perhaps this is because looking younger is no joking matter or because something that expensive generally isn't considered all that amusing unless it's injected into the lips—and then it's so painful, it makes a bikini wax something you reflect upon longingly and with shorter hair. I do know that women have to look younger longer—in part due to the fact that cragginess doesn't enhance most women's overall appearance, and in part because I don't know that many straight men whose goal is to achieve a kind of dewy teenage appearance. But maybe I don't get around enough.)

There was one other woman on the movie besides Pat McDermott and the continuity "girl," and that was Kay

Freeborn. Kay was married to Stuart Freeborn and they had a son, Graham. All of them worked on the movie doing makeup. Stuart had been doing makeup since the silent films, where a lot of makeup was required, since you couldn't hear the dialogue and how you looked was everything. He appeared to me to be about eighty, so he was probably about fifty-five or sixty. He would tell stories while applying your makeup, while the heat of the larger-than-usual lights warmed you. Kay was largely in charge of my makeup, of course, seeing as we were both women—and in an all-male space-fantasy world, we women had to stick together. But Stuart was also known to do mine on occasion.

Stuart seemed to always have a smile on his face (where else would he have a smile?) while he powdered you down and up. "I remember I was doing Vivien Leigh's makeup for *Fire Over England*, which starred herself and her future husband, Laurence Olivier. They had fallen in love while starring in the picture together—but both of them were still married to other people, so they could only really see one another on the sly or they'd get caught, you know. And there was I—a young man myself then—hard to believe now, I know."

I'd interject here, "No! You look incredible!"

He'd laugh gratefully and continue his story. "Well, you're a nice girl," he'd say, smoothing rouge on my cheek with one of his many sponges.

"No! I'm not! I'm not nice! Ask anyone—they'll tell you!"

"So there I'd be, working on Miss Leigh's lipstick for nigh on two hours—for the film was being shot in Technicolor and the lips had to be very red but the skin slightly gray."

I grimaced. "*Gray?!*"

Stuart laughed as he moved to my other cheek. "'Twas to do with the four-step color process of Technicolor. They don't use it these days—too complicated." My eyebrows were next to receive his cinematic enhancement. "So there I am. It took me all of two hours to do Miss Leigh's lips just right, and don't you know, I'm just about finished and there she is, camera ready, and who comes in but his lordship. Only he wasn't his lordship then, of course, he was just that new actor Larry Olivier. Most called him Larry then—but to strangers or fans he was Laurence Olivier, up-and-coming star-to-be. Whatever you called him, though, he came and swooped down, kissing her then and there. All my work—hours of it, like I told you—out the window, and nothing for it but to start all over again."

He shrugged. "Nothin' to be done about it. They were in love and that's all there was to it. You're only young once, so they tell me. Shame, but there it is."

carrison

I've spent so many years not telling the story of Harrison and me having an affair on the first *Star Wars* movie that it's difficult to know exactly how to tell it now. I suppose I'm writing this because it's forty years later and whoever we were then—superficially at least—we no longer are now. Whoever I might've infuriated then wouldn't have the energy to be infuriated now. And even if they did, I wouldn't have the energy to feel as guilty as I would have thirty or twenty or—well, there's no way I could've written it even ten years ago.

There's not much in my life that I've kept secret. Many would argue there are certain otherwise-private stories I might've been wiser to keep closer to the vest. That vest that knows no proximity.

But Carrison is something I've only vaguely alluded to in the past forty years. Why? Why not blather on about this like I've blathered on about everything else? Was it the one thing I wanted to know all by myself—well, me and Harrison? I can only speculate. Anyway there are rules about kissing and telling, aren't there? I'd like to think those only apply to men. And Harrison's been very good about not talking about his half of the story. But just because he's been good doesn't mean that I have to continue to be. Mum is the word for just so long and then it has to go back to being a British parent.

Of course, I didn't feel truly comfortable telling the story before now—and still don't, and probably still won't at whatever point in the future that you're actually reading this—not only because I'm not necessarily a comfortable person in general, but because Harrison was married at the time, and also because really, why would you tell other people about something like that unless you were one of those people who tell everybody everything, not caring about how a particular revelation might affect anyone else who appears in the story?

Not that I've ever done a single thing that might encourage people to consider me anything remotely like the soul of discretion. It's true that I do tell a lot. Indeed, I have the well-deserved reputation of divulging conspicuously more information that would ordinarily fall on the intimate side. But, though I do admittedly lay bare far more than the average bear, before disclosing anything that is possibly someone else's secret to tell, I make it a practice to first let that person know about my intention. (Aren't I ethical? I thought you'd think so.)

They're free to persuade me to alter what I've written to reflect their (obviously gutless) recollection of the experience, or be even more wimpy and ask me to remove them from the story altogether, in light of their concerns that their reputations and/or lives might be forever destroyed. I don't want to make anyone else look stupid. That's a privilege I reserve for myself.

Because, with the exception of fucking with the truth about whether or not I was loaded at any given moment or if I stole painkillers from your medicine cabinet, I'm no liar. I need you to trust that or stop reading. Recollections might differ with regard to the smaller details, but I don't think my perceptions are distorted. No one has ever said to me, "That never happened," or "I don't remember the evening that way *at all*. There were *no* pygmies in our group that night." I mean, if I have even a teensy doubt about something's having happened, then I don't tell the story. Not worth it.

Bottom line, not only am I not a liar, I'm not even an

exaggerator. If anything, I like to dial things down a bit so everything doesn't come off as a drag queen line dance at Mardi Gras.

Do I at times wish I'd had a calmer, wiser, and more manageable sort of existence? One that even at times included pauses and yawning? Absolutely. But then who would I be? More than likely *not* someone who, at nineteen, found herself having an affair with her fourteen-years-older married costar without first ever having had with him a linear, meaningful conversation while clothed.

Also, if I didn't write about it someone else would. Someone without direct knowledge of the "situation." Someone who would wait—cowardly—until after my passing to speculate on what happened and make me look bad. No.

Though no one seems to have any idea that our affair occurred, or even may have occurred, forty years later, here's the truth, the banal, romantic, sweet, awkward truth. The truth that is Carrison.

I began filming *Star Wars* hoping to have an affair. Hoping to strike people as somewhere between sophisticated and louche—someone you'd think had gone to boarding school in Switzerland with Anjelica Huston and had learned to speak four languages, including Portuguese. An affair for a person like that would be a completely predictable and totally adult experience.

This would be my first affair—not surprising, when you think about it, for a nineteen-year-old female in the seventies—and I didn't really know what someone actually needed to do in order to make a thing like that happen. Back then I was always looking ahead to who I wanted to be versus who I didn't realize I already was, and the wished-for me was most likely based on who other people seemed to be and the desire to have the same effect on others that they had had on me.

I knew I was going to be awful with men, partly because of the way my mom had been, with her two divorces and one separation in the pipeline. I possessed that certainty by fifteen or sixteen, and so I needed to prove it to you. Sure, the insight wasn't a comfortable one, but it was *mine*, and I was still young enough to be considered precocious. Wow! I was clairvoyant! Maybe I couldn't fix it, or alter it even a little, but what the hell! I knew what was coming and didn't bother with feeling sorry for my not-too-distant-future self—it might not be great, but I predicted it, named it, claimed it, and tried to project the illusion that I was up to my elbows in control.

Despite the fact that almost everything was new to me then, it was crucial that I appeared to be a kind of nonchalant citizen of the weary part of the world—been there, done not only that but also this, and even that other one a few times later on. I could hardly be expected to do too much more.

Which is undoubtedly why a man might easily have assumed that I'd been around the block, without having any idea how I'd arrived at that block in the first place, or what sort of block it was that I'd been around, and was it lined with homes or trees? Was it an auction block? A city block? Or a chopping one?

I did my best to come off as this kind of ironic, amused, disenchanted creature. An often chatty, even giddy gal with little to no sense of fashion.

Simon Templeman, a British boy I had gone to drama school with, had been my only boyfriend till then, and he and I were together for close to a year before we actually slept together, i.e., had sex. But whatever I'd done or not done with Simon, that—along with some fooling around with three straight guys and kissing three gay guys—was basically the sum total of my earthling version of sexual experience (and an exciting preview of things to come).

Sure, I'd devoted a lot of time to exploring the world of foreplay. Mostly in the shallow end, though—the far reaches caused me, in theory, a certain amount of concern. What if I went there and never made it back? I don't know even still what it was about sex that concerned me. Was it that once you gave up your virginity, that was it—you could never be a virgin again? Ever? Was it that my mother had been known as Tammy? Tammy the Girl Scout, the last one standing at the virgin sit-in, who raised me to be a very good girl, save my milk and not be a cheap cow no one wanted to buy? Or was it my father, the Olympian sex enthusiast?

Maybe it was the specter of the back of my first stepfather Harry Karl's gray, withered hanging ball sack as he rose from the bed without pajama bottoms to yet again visit the bathroom. A ball sack available for my nightly viewing throughout my childhood and on into my adolescence. If that was what my future held—a facsimile of what I would someday have to hold tenderly—I would cling to my blessedly penis- and ball-sack-free present for as long as possible. And that possibility finally ended when Simon and I began.

I am someone who wants very much to be popular. I don't just want you to like me, I want to be one of the most joy-inducing human beings that you've ever encountered. I want to explode on your night sky like fireworks at midnight on New Year's Eve in Hong Kong.

Having famous parents doesn't endear you to your high school classmates. I found this out one day in ninth grade when I overheard two girls walking behind me in the school hallway. One of them said to the other in an audible whisper, "See that girl just ahead of us? With that headband?"

"Yeah?"

"She's Debbie Reynolds's daughter." There was a slight pause before she added, "She thinks she's so great."

Wow, right? Uncanny how she so perfectly nailed me straight out of the box. I just thought I was incredible.

Of course, most people want to be liked, I think, especially when you consider the lonely alternatives. Even the fringier members of society—gangsters, drug cartel types, garden-variety serial killers—even *they* want to be liked in their own endearing ways. They might want to be admired for their own particular brand of impressive awfulness, such as managing to elude the law for longer than anyone in their questionable line of work, or for the unique and even striking manner in which they slaughtered their victims. Clearly there are numerous methods that can be employed in one's ravenous quest to be loved.

Given this desire for popularity, playing the role of "the other woman"—a home wrecker (or even an apartment or lean-to wrecker)—was not on my radar of things to accomplish in a lifetime. I can't think of a single personality trait I have that lends itself to seeking out participation in a sordid situation of that kind.

It's difficult to imagine a childhood less likely to make one pro-adultery than mine. When I was born, my parents, the handsome singer Eddie Fisher and the beautiful actress Debbie Reynolds, were known as "America's Sweethearts." The gorgeous couple with their two adorable little babies (my brother, Todd, came along sixteen months after I did) were the American Dream realized, until Eddie left Debbie for the recently widowed gorgeous actress Elizabeth Taylor, who, just to pile it on a little more, was a friend of my mother's from their early days at the Metro-Goldwyn-Mayer Studio. For those too old to remember or too young to care, it was one of the great midcentury tabloid feeding frenzies, and I watched it at very close range.

At the ripe old age of eighteen months I lost my father to an adulteress. I knew in my heart that the only rationale he could have had for leaving was because of how big a disappointment I must have been, and I wasn't going to do that to some other kid. So it stood to reason that if I could disappoint my own *father*—if I couldn't get my own father to love me enough to stick around or, God forbid, visit more often than one day a year—how was I ever going to get a man who didn't *have* to love me like daddies were supposed to? (Hey, Envious Classmate, see how fucking great I thought I was?)

My first larger-than-life lesson was what it felt like to be on the clueless end of infidelity. So there was absolutely no way—zero!—that I'd carry on that evil tradition of hurting some lovely, unsuspecting lady.

So when I was contemplating having an affair on this movie, I wasn't going to include married guys. (Not that I even thought about not including them.) One of the things I knew when Harrison and I met was that nothing of a romantic nature would happen. It wasn't even an issue. There were plenty of guys out there who were single whom I could date without needing to dip into the married guy pool. He was also far too old for me—almost fifteen years older! I would be twenty in a matter of months, but Harrison was in his midthirties—old! Well into adulthood, anyway.

Also, he was a man. I was a girl—a male human like him would have to be with a woman. If Harrison and I went to the prom together, no one would believe it. "What's he doing with *her*? Captain of the football team and president of the cool literary club? What's he doing with Cutie-Pie Sweetcheeks, with the troll doll collection and Cary Grant obsession? Must be a glitch in the machine..."

On top of that, there was something intimidating about Harrison. His face in repose looked to me like it was closer to a scowl than to any other expression. It was immediately clear that he was no people pleaser; this was more of a people *unsettler*. He looked like he didn't care whether or not you looked at him, so you watched him not caring, hungrily. Anyone with him was irrelevant, and I was definitely an "anyone."

When I'd first seen him sitting on the cantina set, I remember thinking, This guy's going to be a star. Not just a celebrity, a movie star. He looked like one of those iconic Movie Star types, like Humphrey Bogart or Spencer Tracy. Some sort of epic energy hung around him like an invisible throng.

I mean, let's say that you're walking along in the twilight, minding your own business (your own *show* business), and there's fog all around you—a mysterious sort of cinematic fog. And as you continue walking, you find that you're moving slower and slower, because you can barely see a few feet in front of you. And then all of a sudden the smoke clears. It clears enough for you to imagine that you're beginning to ever so slowly make out the outline of the face. And not just a face. This is the face of someone that painters would want to paint or poets would wax poetic about. An Irish balladeer would feel compelled to write a song to be sung drunkenly in pubs all over the United Kingdom. A sculptor would sob openly while carving the scar on his chin.

A face for the ages. And seeing him sitting there in the set that would introduce him to the world as Han Solo, the most famous of all the famous characters that he would come to play—well, he was just so far out of my league. Compared to him I didn't even have an actual verifiable league. We were destined for different places.

Having grown up around show business, I knew that there were stars and there were *stars*. There were celebrities, talk show hosts, product spokespeople, and then there were *movie stars*—people with agents and managers and publicists and assistants and bodyguards, who got tons of fan mail and could get a movie financed, and who consistently graced the covers of magazines. Their grinning familiar faces stared proudly out at you, encouraging you to catch up on their personal lives, their projects, and how close they were to being the most down-to-earth of those famous-to-earthlings.

Harrison was one of that epic superstar variety, and I wasn't. Was I bitter about this? Well... not so you'd notice.

I was in the last year of my teens, only weeks free from my drama college romance and in my first starring movie role. I was extremely insecure. I felt as though I didn't know what I was doing, and for good reason. In most areas, I didn't.

Oh, I could be witty as the deuce, but I had no idea how I should best apply that cleverness, for I was clever, not intellectual. I had very little learned knowledge, having dropped out of high school to be a chorus girl in my mother's Broadway show, and I was very insecure about my lack of education. I was a voracious reader, but part of what that taught me was that I was nowhere near as scholarly as I wanted to be. I was precocious, but how many years beyond your teens can you be called that with sincerity?

I was good with words and had an ability to analyze people and things, but only enough for a party trick—at least that's what I told myself at the time. I would tell you I wasn't as smart as you thought I was, but obviously not without first establishing that you thought I was bright. Still, knowing that I was insecure, I couldn't imagine being with someone who seemed to be overconfident. But then, was Harrison *over*confident if it transpired that his high opinion of himself was based on a clear-eyed assessment?

It was all so confusing. But one thing I knew was that Harrison made me feel very nervous. I got tongue-tied in his company, and clumsy. It was uncomfortable in the extreme, and not in any way I could overcome with a few well-chosen witticisms. We met, hit a wall, and stayed there. It didn't seem like a challenge, it seemed like something to avoid whenever possible. I was with him when we worked in scenes together and I tried to avoid him otherwise so as not to annoy him—not to, as it felt like to me, waste his better-spent time. It was more comfortable to hang out with the cast and crew who were more fun and less immune to my charms.

But when I look back with squinting eyes, I figure Harrison was scoping out the set in those early days. Not to have an affair necessarily, but then again, not *not* to either. We were on location, after all, and to have a little quiet jaunt on the side wasn't the worst thing he could do. It was almost expected. On location—far from home...

So while I combed the environs for my potential location adventure, Harrison may have been combing, too.

On one of the first Friday nights after filming began, a party was organized to celebrate George Lucas's thirty-second birthday. It was billed as a surprise party, though I'd be surprised if he was actually surprised by it. And even if he was, you never knew with George. He really wasn't into facial expressions, much like Darth Vader and various and sundry robots, stormtroopers, and Ewoks.

One thing George never did like other directors—I was to later learn, with dismay—was encourage us to "just have fun with it." So many directors have urged me in that amused direction, and I always want to say, "Is that what I'm here for? Fun? I am here for my salary, and to periodically use an ill-advised British accent, and to get people that I don't know to like me." Fun was for later, and generally misguided, which brings me back to George's surprise party.

The festivities took place in a medium-sized, uncluttered room adjacent to the cafeteria at Elstree Studios. The walls were dirty-yellow, though a more generous and myopic guest might call it mustard. Most of the assembled crowd was made up of the crew—the grips, the electricians ("sparks" in the UK), the drivers, and all the others who toiled daily on the new, fairly obscure film that was being shot there. If they can get on the screen half of what George put on the page, I thought, people will come to see it. No matter what, it's going to be this cool, weird little movie. I'd go see it. Well, I'd have to anyway, but they wouldn't have to drag me.

So, this cafeteria was a biggish blank sort of place—inscrutable, impassive, without affect, the better that you might concentrate on what you were ingesting, which would have been chips, dips, carrots, celery, and pretzels. And next to the table boasting this decidedly less-than-exciting spread was everybody's destination, another table with more sought-after treasures: the bar.

Not having located George yet, I tried to look as unconcerned and blasé as possible as I slowly sauntered barward, adding a smile to the mix in order to make it easier for the people there to like me and not wonder why I, of all people, had been cast in the role of the rather daunting princess.

"Hi! How you doing?" What was *his* name? "Great to see you." Oh, no—what was *his* name? What were *any* of their names, I wondered as I weaved through this ever-growing crowd of faces I saw every day. Of course, they all knew my name because there it was on the call sheet.

"Could I have a Coke with ice, please? In as big a glass as you've got? Oh, that's right, we're in England, there is no ice. Okay, then, warm Coke it is."

And then there was Harrison at the door. Wow, he really looked *thrilled* to be there. It could happen, though, I thought. This could be the night that he smiles. I waved as I brought my warm cola to my lips, hoping it wasn't *that* warm. Not swamp-in-summer or overheated-hot-tub warm. Harrison raised his hand in a gesture intended as a greeting and began making his way through the assembled group that was every minute growing larger—a social fungus, slowly and deliberately fed by the bar.

"Sure, I remember you!" I emphatically reassured someone else whom I again didn't remember. "Yeah! I'm having a great time. Are you?"

"Hey, look who's here," I greeted another. "I wondered if you'd be coming. No, I'm not, I really wondered! No, I already have a drink. It does so pass for a drink. Alcohol isn't the only thing that quenches thirst. It's the sense-quenching component that baffles me. Say that three times fast: Sense-quenching. Sense-quenching. Sense-quenching. No, really, I can't drink. I've tried, I really have given it my best shot. But really, I'm allergic to booze. It makes me stupid, sick, and unconscious really fast. So I've never actually been drunk—just senseless and inert. I love that word, don't you? 'Inert.'"

The gathering smoke transformed this nondescript accommodation into the back room of a pub near closing time—all that was missing was the pool table. Following a somewhat shy beginning, everyone came to realize that this was not some polite celebration for their forbidding boss who was all but unknown to them. This was a kind of gleeful car wreck taking place at the end of a long early-in-the-shoot week. Maybe we were already behind schedule.

A lot of the crew knew each other from other shoots, and the filming—except for a brief jaunt to Tunisia—was taking place at home. No uprooting and staying at some cheap but comfortable faraway hotel. Most of these folks would go home at the end of a workday/week/month and sit at their own dinner tables, surrounded by their loving, supportive families, and beam with barely suppressed joy at the spouse or family who took a lively interest in his or her day.

Indeed, this very issue was being discussed. "This ain't

nobody round here's idea of fun and frolic in the workplace, right?" a crew member said. "Everyone I've ever worked with that's got a brain in their bloody head would rather be in some warm nowhere-near-here spot—say, on the coast someplace where the locals are ready and willing and the ale is dark and flowing."

"Home?" said another. "After working all the livelong day on some dark set waiting for the bell so's you can talk above a whisper—fuck me five ways till Friday. Give me a nice remote location with some per diem to pay for a round or two in the local bar, where there's no bloody shortage of strange but friendly quim, and we're off to the races, eh, lads?"

Meanwhile, two members of the crew—the second assistant directors Terry and Roy—began making sport with me. "Look who we have here, boys! It's our little princess without her buns!"

I think part of their motive was that I was essentially the only girl at this party, and it would be more entertaining to have the only girl at a party completely off-her-ass drunk than not. If it was the last thing they did, they were going to get me to drink some of that hard liquor everyone was guzzling. It became one of the main focuses of the night—let's get Leia legless—and if I played along, it would be the most idiotic choice I could make, considering that this shindig would no doubt include everyone I knew on the film, including my bosses, the producers, and the birthday boy himself, the director.

A kind of bawdy Victorian interaction ensued, much in the vernacular. Any people who use language the way the British do—with colloquialisms like "twat" (rhymes with "fat") and "cunt" (rhymes with everything) at their core—how could you ever tire of listening to and/or interacting with such a gang?

Well, perhaps you can, but I never have. I fell in love with London while I was at school there and have never fallen out. I love their being as bound up in their history as they are, preserving their buildings instead of razing them to the ground to make way for another big beige building with lots of windows to throw yourself screaming from. I love its accents, its exchange rates, its idiosyncratic friendly behavior, its museums, its parks you need keys for, and its colas without ice. If I can forgive a place for not making ice a priority as part of their lifestyle, that's true love.

We all banded together and sang a hideous version of "Happy Birthday," after which Harrison began a conversation with George. I was once again surrounded by a musty, sweat-scented, denim-and-T-shirt-clad crowd of heterosexual men. Whether it was muscle or fat that filled out their unremarkable T-shirts, they all looked various degrees of attractive to me, in part because a lot of them actually *were* attractive and in part because of how undeniably attractive I looked to them, just shy of being an underage girl. But come on, me, give me some credit! I wasn't merely all that was available on the menu—I was nineteen and cute as the deuce. I can see that now, though if you asked me then, I would have said I was fat faced with a chunky body.

They kept pushing for me to have a drink, and finally the people pleaser in me took over and I agreed to let one of the crew get me one. I asked for an amaretto, the only thing I drank. It tastes like awful cough syrup—which is redundant—but at least it would be a familiar taste. I didn't have a cough or sore throat, I rationalized, but maybe I could prevent one from coming on. One of the special effects crew cheered at my acquiescence.

"I don't know how anyone can drink alcohol, just based on the taste," I said. "It's like rust. I've seen people swirl wine in their mouths with delight and it baffles me."

"Me, too, luv," one of the crew replied. "I'm in it for the effect is all—screw the taste."

"Yeah, but when I was young, it looked so great to me—people standing around in clusters, drinks in hand, heads thrown back in wild laughter—and I just couldn't wait for that to happen to me. I couldn't wait to learn the secret of alcohol that unleashes all that gaiety from deep within. But it was a lie, a horrible, horrible lie, and someone is someday going to have to pay for it."

"Look here, my darling," said the crew member who'd returned from the bar. "No one is going to have to pay for this—it's courtesy of George Lucas."

I looked at the glass he handed me, but instead of finding amaretto, I discovered a glass of what I assumed was wine. I frowned.

"Sorry, luvvie, they didn't have your fancy sweet drink," the crew member said. "But this should do what amaretto does and one better."

Why did I drink it? Maybe to show them how bad an idea alcohol was for me. But whatever the reason, the bottom line is that I drank. My face went into a tight-fisted grimace after my first swig of the foul stuff. And another swig, and another after that. I couldn't focus on the taste for very long, because there I was laughing, laughing like those adults I watched at my mother's parties when I was a kid.

"Remember that first week when we did the swing across?" I said.

"What's a swing across, mate?"

"I'm telling you! I'm trying to tell you! It was when Mark and I swung on a rope from that platform thing to the other side! You know! You know what I mean!"

They did. Not that the crew cared about my story, they only cared that I continued to drink, which I did. They laughed at whatever I said, and I appreciated their laughter, and so continued down that same path until the lines of that path became increasingly blurry and whether it was or wasn't a path at all mattered less. Everything mattered less. What mattered most was that we continued laughing and had a good time.

I don't know when I became aware that quite a few members of the crew were organizing a kind of joke abduction of me. I don't know this because quite a lot of time has transpired between George's surprise party forty years ago and now.

It was a jovial sort of a plan. To get me out of the party and take me away to wherever movie crews take young actresses when they want to establish that the actress belongs to them, at least for the moment, and not to any cast members or production folk. Certainly it wasn't a serious thing. What made it look serious was how big the men tended to be in some of the various factions.

At some point I realized my head was hurting. Not hurting exactly, it just felt different than it usually did, which I mentioned.

"You need to get some air," one of the crew said.

"Isn't there air in here?" I said. "What have I been breathing then?"

"Hey," a new voice called out as I was being steered toward an available door by a few of the friendlier sparks. The sparks were sparking to me, weren't they? We were just about to pass through the door when I heard that voice again. An American one, not British. A Yankee voice. "Where are you taking her?"

"Nowhere, man, the lady just wants to get a little air is all."

"Pardon me, but the lady doesn't seem to be very aware of what she wants." Then I knew who it was. Harrison! My costar! What was he saying? I didn't know what I wanted? That might have been true, but when did he become the expert on what I did or didn't want?

"Hey, Harrison!" I greeted him as he found his way to my circle. "Where've you been?"

I have no idea what these rowdy Brits thought they were going to do with me. I have to believe not much, but they were going to make a lot of noise while they didn't do it. And Harrison was suddenly making a great show of saving me from what I can only guess at. (But why bother?) The crew pulled, Harrison pushed back, I tried to stay in focus.

But there was also an element of danger. Not with a capital "D" but the word in whatever form applies due to the roughhousing that seemed to rule the day, or the roost, or the world. What began as a kind of pretend stage-fight tug-of-war transformed into a more earnest battle for a woman's—what is the word?—maidenhood. No! Virtue! A tug-of-war involving my wine-sodden virtue was under way and I was unclear how it would all turn out. But vaguely interested, and that's a fact.

Once I could wrap what remained of my mind around who was involved in this tug-of-war, I gradually came to realize who it was that I wanted to win: my costar, the smuggler, the one with the scar on his chin, the dialogue in his head, and the gun in his belt—not now, just when in character, but still . . . I felt the gun was implied and so must've the crew, because after a mad scuffle, which left Harrison limping, Mr. Ford threw my virtue and me into the backseat of his studio car and commanded the driver to "Go! GO!" We went, followed on foot for the briefest but boldest of times by the film set crew—the finest of men.

About halfway to London from Elstree, I heard the honking of a horn. That is, I eventually realized that's what the persistent noise was. I pushed Harrison's shoulder back. "What's that?" I asked, panicked. "Is someone honking?"

"Shit," mumbled Harrison, squinting out the back car window over my head. "It's Mark and Peter."

"Oh my God." I started to sit up, but he stopped me with his hand and voice.

"Fix your hair."

My hair, my hair, my hair—it was always my hair with this movie, on-screen or off. I stayed slunk down while I did my unlevel best to straighten my hair and then slowly rose, afraid of who I'd find out the window, and would they be armed? Armed with a camera and shocked face? Or . . . ?

"Just act normal," Harrison suggested. Realizing that acting normal would take *hours* and a team of horses, I grinned and waved at the two of them through the window, the closest I could get to normal without assistance, additional encouragement, and a hat. "They were sort of behind us so they couldn't have seen anything."

While I watched, a blue car caught up with us on our right. One of the crew, Peter Kohn, was driving the car, with a beautiful girl to the left of him in the passenger seat, the actress Koo Stark. Mark was in the backseat, leaning all the way forward into the front seat between Peter and the girl. He waved happily and smiled. I waved back and showed them my upper teeth.

I watched Harrison roll down his window of the car. This was prehistoric England; windows were lowered manually, phones had to be dialed, and everything was closed on Sunday by eleven o'clock at night. And when I say "everything," I mean *everything*. It amazed me.

Plus they didn't sell corn bread, most breakfast cereals, pancake mix, pinto beans, or regular bacon! That was my staple diet! How did people *survive*? There were tons of ordinary American products that couldn't be purchased in the UK. Some of them could be found at Fortnum & Mason on Piccadilly. I knew all of this from having already lived in London for the last few years. The Americans who made up our cast (Mark and Harrison) and crew (George and Gary et al.) on *Star Wars* were just finding it out.

One of those Americans was the previously mentioned Peter Kohn, who usually wore a knit hat and long dark blue or maroon sweaters. Exactly what services he provided to *Star Wars* I wasn't exactly sure. He didn't seem to be there in any sort of normal official capacity, not that I would really know what a normal official capacity looked like, but here we were, Peter, Koo Stark, and the stars of the movie, all on our way to the same restaurant.

The fact that Harrison and I had rolled around in the backseat during our return to London didn't necessarily mean that it was a prologue for a more elaborate event. An inkling of what was coming, maybe. Sure, there had been some unexpected exploratory kissing: reading another person's face with your mouth with dedicated eagerness, swimming with your lips between a particular person's nose and chin, gently digging for jewels using your tongue as a makeshift shovel, jewels buried in the mouth of your beloved—wait! I think I felt a sapphire over here near the back molar on the left. Fishing face-to-face—like grouper, but without the water, the scales, and that awful fishy smell. But otherwise...

Kissing that way doesn't necessarily sound like something I'd have been eager to do on a regular basis. Once a month maybe, under the right circumstances, which might include the drive from the studio to the city. It might have been the purr of the motor that got us there.

But get there we did somehow, having dinner with Mark, Peter, and Koo Stark—whose work in *Star Wars* tragically ended up on the cutting room floor—and who should avoid leaving things (e.g., purses) at people's houses so they don't have to hold the thing aloft and wonder aloud, "Does anyone know who this belongs to?" and ignite a chorus of the reply, "I think that's Koo's." No matter how pretty she was (and undoubtedly continues to be), no one escapes a splash of the ridiculous when referred to in the possessive as "Koo's."

So I'm at a restaurant in London, with most of my thoughts centered on how much prettier Koo is than me, how confident she seems to be—obviously in part due to her beauty. I wonder if she's having an affair with Peter and assume that she more than likely is, because Peter is attractive also. Not as attractive as Koo, but he doesn't have to be because as you no doubt are aware, if you have a penis and a job, being handsome is a fantastic bonus but hardly a necessity.

So Koo was with Peter in all likelihood. Mark was alone, and Harrison was... Harrison was on his lickety-split way to being pretty much everything to me. He would all too soon become the center of my off-center, kilter-free world. Which, I agree absolutely, is pathetic in the extreme—but keep in mind that this whole thing was *not* my weirdly inexperienced idea. It was Harrison's. I was just some innocent bystander doing her not-exactly-levelheaded best to burn off the alcohol she had ingested earlier that evening. Maybe then I could make *some* sense of what had happened in the car with Harrison—not what had happened so much as would it ever happen again? And if so, would that be on the soon side? Now that the offer was essentially on the table, would it *stay* on the table or continue onto the bed?

I don't recall much about that dinner except how incredibly self-conscious I was, how awkward and fuzzy I felt from having consumed two and a half glasses of an alcoholic beverage. And not even *hard* liquor—the sort that's as dense and inscrutable as cement. This was the softer variety of alcohol, floaty, giggly, and vague. I attempted to counter these inconvenient blur-encouraging effects by combating them with large quantities of my all-purpose sugary, caffeinated, carbonated healing elixir—Coca-Cola. I hoped I would feel its rallying effects *very* soon.

I drank a few restorative rounds of Coke and tried very hard to not look at Harrison. How could I? What would he think if he caught me looking at him? That I liked him? Ugh, in that awful embarrassing way that's impossible to hide? And, this was totally his fault. He was the one who started making out in the back of the car. I would never have considered liking him, left to my own devices. What devices? How many did I have? Had I had them long? What if what I assumed were devices were, in fact, delusions? So, more accurate to ask, "Left to my own delusions, would I have been able to convince myself that I wasn't suddenly infatuated with Harrison?"

Fresh Coke in hand notwithstanding, I was still a little drunk—an altered state that I was inordinately unaccustomed to. Stoned, I knew. Cheerfully bleary-eyed from the effects of pot—yes, that I was not only used to but got increasingly used to as time went on. Used to in a great way. Under the shade of its effects, subjects I had formerly considered barely worth noticing could now both catch my eye and keep it.

Alcohol was another matter. A dark, regrettable experience that I always promised myself (and/or whoever else might be listening) I would never go near again if whoever had the most pull in the area of intoxication would let me off easy. Yet, here I was again.

Seated at our table, I figured it would be all right to look at Harrison when and if he said something, but my hair could grow if I waited for that unlikely event, right?

Wrong. That evening he talked more than I'd ever seen him talk. There were stories about the day we'd had an early call—hardly unusual—and by early afternoon we still hadn't been summoned to the set to film anything. "It doesn't bother me that much to be kept waiting," Mark volunteered as he sprinkled cheese over his pasta. "Obviously I don't like it, but there are ways to keep yourself entertained."

"Oh, yeah," drawled Mr. Ford, "what are those ways? Catching up on your correspondence or taking up the zither." I listened intently—everything depended on my getting into this conversation while trying to convey that it didn't matter to me at all.

"I would pay many hard-earned dollars to see you play the zither," I offered shyly, hyperaware of making a good impression.

Harrison studied me briefly from his prime real estate across the table. He slowly rubbed his chin with his left hand while he considered my offer. He pursed his lips and began tapping them very slowly. Narrowing his hazel eyes, he said, "How much?"

He waited for my reply calmly, knowingly—he wasn't smiling, but he wasn't *not* smiling either. Under the table, I picked at the skin on my thumb, ripping off a strand, suddenly lost. What were we talking about? Why was he looking at me like that? Did I have food on my face? I looked at the other people at the table—coincidentally they were *all* looking at me as well! Why was everyone looking at me? I *must* have food on my face. I wiped the corners of my mouth with my now-slightly-bleeding hand.

"How much for what?" I asked them sadly. "I'm a little lost, what scene is this?" Now I sounded as if I was pleading. Not for my life necessarily, but for a way to live it nobly—like a poet on a porch.

They laughed when I asked what scene it was. Harrison didn't laugh, but he looked as though he might have if he'd been made a different way. Then I remembered, at least part of it.

"Play the zither! I'm going to pay you to play the zither!"

"Now?" Harrison said.

"Yes!"

That was the first I had laughed. We all laughed. Maybe everything would be all right now. Sure! That was it! It was a sign! It all started and ended with the zither. And something else, too—I was going to go home with Harrison. I wasn't sure up until that moment, and I wasn't sure of what would happen after I went home with him. I knew it wasn't a good idea. It would never be a good idea, but it wouldn't be a really bad one either. I mean, weird and grumpy as he might have been, he wasn't a bad human. He was much more on the good side of the bad/good human graph. He was bad and good, like most people. A good person who does bad things or a bad person who does good things—as long as people are involved, people will do bad or good things to them. Especially when there's money (and small dogs) involved.

The check was fought for valiantly by all us available good soldiers, understanding as we did on some dark and smiling level that those blessed with a bounty of backed-up semen would actually pay it. Koo and I played at being semi-cloyingly grateful for the gallant sacrifice of their hard-won shekels and we rose from our four-sided trough, thus easing our way out of our eatery and on to the finer events that no doubt awaited us all.

I was in no shape to do anything but take cues, when and if they were distributed with intent. But perhaps I had misread the situation—was I following a lead that only existed in my unaccustomed-to-alcohol-and-as-such-altered mind? But I was slowly sobering up, and the likelihood that I was misreading signals was getting lower by the minute as we stood on the sidewalk outside the little Italian restaurant I'd so recently managed to survive. The cool air was welcome—who knew that there was so much of it outside! Especially when compared to the overall quantity of air set aside for eateries.

We stood under the timid light of a nearby street lamp, shuffling from one foot to the other, checking watches, lighting cigarettes, or squinting into the night to ascertain whether or not there were any incoming cabs.

"I'm in Chelsea," Mark said.

"So you decided to keep that place in the end?" Peter observed, nodding wisely.

Mark shrugged. "In the end I figured, why not? It's got great views, an awesome kitchen... I mean, sure there are better neighborhoods, but . . ." He paused and shrugged again. "But not with a second bedroom."

Harrison flicked away his barely smoked Camel and coughed. "Okay!" he said to everyone. He then looked at me. "I can drop you at your place—it's on my way."

He took my arm and steered me toward Piccadilly Circus.

"Good night!" I managed as Harrison drew me along into the street and away from them. That I didn't stumble was a miracle, not like the virgin birth or anything, but you could've fooled me. We walked in silence for several moments while I riffed through an assortment of remarks I might make, enabling me to seem . . . to seem like someone . . . a woman even, who knew what she was doing—or didn't care what she was doing—because wherever she went only the very best people would follow. Follow her every word like welcome stalkers—why wouldn't Harrison want to be where she was? If only she felt this way about herself, if only she could think of what to say to him—other than ask him what they were doing. Where were they going and why? Would he ask her to the prom and cover her in hickeys?

Now, of course she loved him, didn't she? She wouldn't have dared to before that business in the backseat, but now . . .

"What's your address?" he asked, startling me, standing there beside this king, Han Solo and all the other characters he would eventually play seeded in him now. And then there was me, pregnant with all those people I would play: a vengeful hairdresser, a hostile mother-in-law, a flute-playing adulteress, a psychologist, a drug-addicted writer, a boyfriend-poaching actress, a boy-hungry casting director, myself, an unfaithful wife, an angry boss, myself, myself, myself, myself, and a couple of nuns. He took me by the elbow and eased all of us into the backseat of a taxi.

"What's your address?"

I looked at him, blinking. "My address?"

"Where we going, ladies and gents?" The driver put the taxi in gear and it growled back to life. "Or I could drive you kids around all night, it's your money."

Harrison nodded in agreement, twirling his index finger rapidly—the international indicator to hurry things along.

"Fine, Esmond Court, off Kensington High Street."

"Okay, lady. Have you there in a jiff," he all but cheered in his cockney Dick Van Dyke East London accent. The one I wish I had. "That's behind Barkers, is it?"

I was about to tell him when Harrison pulled me back into the seat, moving us closer and closer together, face-to-face, until we were two faces, four eyes, one kiss, going to the place where we could rehearse that kissing we would be doing a year and a half later in *The Empire Strikes Back*—and apparently we wanted to get a jump on it, as it were. People think you just kiss in a love scene. They don't realize the years some actors put into those scenes. Real actors. All that practice really shows. But you don't have to take my word for it. Check out those kisses in *Empire*. See? Those were years in preparation and I promise you, they did not have to use special effects there. These were the early days and nights of the Force.

"Here we are, folks! Esmond Court!" This was punctuated by the sharp sound of the pulled brake. "That'll be five pound ten please."

Harrison reached around to retrieve his brown beat-up

wallet from his back pocket. I pulled my bag from the floor and into my lap, saying, "I could—"

He looked at me indicating that what remained of the sentence I had started would be less than welcome. I may have become a blush factory, sending southerly blood to my northerly face for a visit. It now occurred to me—belatedly, I admit—that Harrison wasn't just dropping me off, but that we were very likely going to be having what my friends and I referred to as a sleepover. What if he—if we—and then—oh God—then he would leave me with my new slutty sense of myself established in one fell swoop—a fallen woman flat on her face, swooping for all she was worth... Leia would never get in a situation like this...

Actually she probably would, but not until the sequels. This was sequel behavior. Oh, but what if she did get into the backseat of a taxi with a smuggling married actor? If she did happen to do that, she wouldn't just go along with things like a leaf on a rushing stream. C'mon! She'd be able to come up with something more unusual . . . maybe not poetic but... Why was I so obedient? What would Leia do? Obviously it would be different than following Jesus's example. Jesus would hardly—well, it's no use pursuing Jesus's lead when it came to dating. And is that what this was? Dating? Oh, Leia, where are you when I need you? Oh, Jesus, if you're watching, please don't let my stomach look other than flat if it should get to that.

"Cheers, mate," the cabbie said as Harrison paid the fare. He then drove off, leaving us in something better than a lurch.

"You wanna come up?" I asked absurdly.

He almost laughed. "Sure."

I reached in my bag for my keys. Leia found them and led him into the building to her apartment, and Carrie spent the rest of the night making sequels with her future cinematic husband. How would it all end? Would it all end? And how would I look when it did?

It's difficult to recall with any kind of clarity details from that weekend. Even if I could, what are we talking about here, soft porn for hardened sci-fi fans? I can't remember events from yesterday, or earlier tonight when I put away my credit cards for safekeeping. Now for the life of me I don't know precisely what safekeeping is.

What I do know about that weekend is more along the lines of what didn't happen. I know we didn't have any in-depth conversations about anything. So if we didn't spend a bunch of time talking or playing Monopoly, then we must've done more physical things. Long walks, water-boarding, things of that nature.

Oh, but why be coy or discreet? We had a sleepover—you know, like we made a fort with pillows after we had a really big pillow fight, then we called his mom and got permission for him to stay overnight, but we couldn't stay up too late, because we had school on Monday, and besides which we were in the school play. All I can remember after he followed me into the apartment and turned on the hallway light was that I meant to show him around my little flat, only now our fumbling was not in a moving vehicle, driven by a knowing spectator. We were once again practicing for our cinematic snog.

The bedroom couldn't get dark enough; even with the lights off I still wanted to turn the lights out. I didn't want him to recognize me from the movies. "Hey! Weren't you in . . . that scene we shot today? Don't I know you from . . . Cloud City?"

Okay, so now we'd spoken together with our words, we'd bantered together using George's words—now we were exploring the outer reaches of no speak, of memorizing the bottom of each other's faces with our mouths. If you'd told me that morning when my bed was being used for other purposes that—well, if I didn't know *Star Wars* was going to be that big of a hit, how could I have predicted that the stars of *Star Wars* would find themselves in bed together?

I don't believe people are across-the-board confident. If they are . . . well, they've misjudged the situation where there's an arrogant result. Mostly people have those few things they do well and hope those things make up for the other shit.

Why am I telling you this? Partly because with my combination of insecurity and inexperience I was paralyzed. Scared to say anything that might make Harrison leave me in the lurch that had all too recently been Riggs's apartment. A tiny part of me felt like I'd won the man lottery and here I was both counting and spending the money. Our skin agreed. We pressed our luck—first his, then mine, then ours—until we had smoothed our way into the thick of it, until nothing else was possible except to get through to each other, in and on through each other, until we eased into the other side.

I looked over at Harrison. He was... God, he was just so handsome. No. No, more than that. He looked like he could lead the charge into battle, take the hill, win the duel, be leader of the gluten-free world, all without breaking a sweat. A hero's face—a few strands of hair fell over his noble, slightly furrowed brow—watching the horizon for danger in the form of incoming indigenous armies, reflective, concerned eyes so deep in thought you could get lost down there and it would take days to fight your way out. But why run? It couldn't really be a hardship to find yourself lost in such a place with all that wit and ideas safely stored there. Hey, man! Wait a second! Share the wealth here. Give the face to one man and save the mind for another and both would have plenty. But no! This was the ultimate living example of overkill. So how could you ask such a shining specimen of a man to be satisfied with the likes of me? No! Don't tell me! The fact is that he was! Even if it was for a short while. That was way more than enough. It would eventually get to be exhausting trying to measure up, or keep up. I was a lucky girl—without the self-esteem to feel it, or the wherewithal to enjoy what there was to enjoy of it and then let go. Only to look back on it forty years on with amused, grateful, and all-but-puffy eyes.

Suffice it to say, we survived and then some. Difficult from this distance to know how close our close was, and whether this brand of close had as much to do with the proximity of someone who looked so very much like my space date—he who smirked at me while jumping to light speed (while I required no assistance whatsoever).

Our affable ordeal behind us, Harrison fell asleep and I tried to. God, he really *was* handsome. I forgave him for not loving me in the way one usually expects—and almost forgave myself for not expecting it. I tried to follow him into slumber land, and when I couldn't, I breathed with him there in the dark—wondering what he was dreaming and hoping that if I actually managed to fall asleep, in the morning, I would wake up before he did. Maybe I'd be better at talking with him now—less daunted, in character and out.

There are some things that I still consider private.

Amazing, isn't it? You would think, without concentrating too hard, that I consider whatever I said and did up for grabs. Way up where the grabs are groped the most. But sex is private. That might be one reason we do it—for the most part—in the nude. Clothes falling away signals a situation that I'll likely avoid putting into words. If clothes don't dress it up, don't expect talk to, either.

So it is with uncharacteristic reservation and scruples that I quash any details, put the kibosh on sharing anything but the most general information or description hereinafter when relating what occurred between Mr. Ford and me on that fateful Friday night in May 1976. This applies also to whatever it was that occurred between Harrison and me on subsequent Fridays at ungodly hours. For that is when we spent our time together, when we had our sleepovers, like good youngsters do. Oh, we spent time together during daylight hours following our time together at night. Such as it was. I think I recall his reading the paper while I... while I pretended to do something else.

Privacy questions aside, I can barely recall our time together during our first weekend. I didn't know how I would live through the five whole days of filming following that first weekend. Those five days on set together went unbearably slowly, with our having to behave toward each other as though the weekend before hadn't even occurred. Weekdays were off-limits, intimacy-wise. Not that this had ever been expressly stated by either one of us. We simply intuited we would spend our weekdays treating one another as though not only had that first weekend not happened, but all of the ensuing ones hadn't happened either.

Despite the common use of the phrase "going out with" to describe two people spending time together, Harrison and I didn't spend a lot of time going out, or wouldn't.

Instead, we went into each other's apartments. I remember spending most of our weekends together at my rented domain in Esmond Court, but that could just be where my memory goes when I send it back to the seventies. I know I wanted to spend our time together there and not at his place.

I preferred Harrison staying over at my apartment because—as the borrowed flat of a friend of mine—it was nicer than his. Sorry, but it was. We all received scale for the first film, which amounted to about $500 a week. And while I came from a wealthy family (though of recently reduced circumstances) and could have afforded rent for nice accommodations even if I hadn't been able to borrow Riggs's flat, Harrison had a wife and two children at home, so in order to maintain their support, he lived in the most modest housing that the studio could get away with providing him. So when it came down to where we would stay, the choice became fairly obvious soon enough.

Once, on one of the rare occasions when we did have a sleepover at Harrison's apartment, Mark and his fairly ubiquitous friend Peter dropped by unannounced. It was about eleven o'clock in the morning, and it might have looked odd that I was there. Clearly I hadn't just dropped by for brunch, as no scones or eggs were in evidence, and we didn't appear to be running lines. Harrison, after letting Mark in, returned to the table we'd been sitting at, sat down across from me, took my hand, and pronounced solemnly, "We're engaged." It was hiding in plain sight, mocking the suggestion that there was anything going on; therefore, it couldn't be true—a technique I like to use to this day.

But I also know that I wasn't good at being clear about anything that I wanted with Harrison. I could charm the birds out of everyone's trees but his. That's something I wrote in the diaries that I kept during the filming of *Star Wars*. The first one, *Episode IV*. The diaries I found recently while expanding my bedroom at home. I was going through the many boxes that were stored romantically beneath the floorboards and came across three written notebooks I had kept during that epic time—and then promptly forgot I'd kept. Or that they kept me, in some ways, sane.

When I read them, I was struck by how unusual they were, which is when I first considered publishing them. (I still might. What do you think?)

There were two reasons that I wrote the diaries, the first one being that I'd always written, since I was about twelve. It seemed to calm me, getting anything that might be chaotic behind the eyes onto the page in front of me where it could do me less harm. Along the lines of the saying, "Better out than in," though that refers to vomit. Maybe more like, "Better an empty house than an unhappy tenant." Not that writing on my notepads managed to actually empty my mind—though some would argue—but I was grateful to relieve the overflow.

The second reason I wrote them was that I couldn't talk to Harrison. Basically about anything, but especially about the entity that was "us"—not that there actually was such a thing. Not only couldn't I converse with Harrison, but given that my weekends with Harrison were a secret, it became something that was better left unsaid, to discuss, only with my pen in hand, with the journal in front of me. I felt that I couldn't confide in anyone else what was happening with Harrison, because Harrison was married. And not to me.

So it might get awkward if I told a person about us, because then that person might tell someone else, and that person would tell another person until eventually Harrison's wife might hear about it and react other than positively about it in the extreme. And nobody wanted that. Not that Harrison and I had ever discussed not wanting it. It was an understood not-wanting.

I think that might be an overall understanding one arrives at, either verbally or otherwise, when you're having an affair with someone who is unaccountably a married person, unless perhaps the wedded individual tells you that his wife doesn't understand him, which is why he wants to leave her to be with you. Or, in this instance, me. And no one was telling anyone that they felt misunderstood and as such there wouldn't be anything leaving-wise in this instance. So that was that.

I only know about the understandings you have with married men and such from movies or books. Never had an affair with a married man, that was me. I'd barely had understandings with a single man. And I've never been with someone wedded since. As I may have mentioned, I had really only had a relationship of any sort with one human being prior to my being with Harrison.

But Harrison didn't know that right away. All he knew was . . . essentially nothing prior to our initial weekend of untold romance and unforgettable passion. I mean, you know, general stuff that you write on forms. Name. Parents. Siblings. Friends. Schools. Plus, anecdotes intended no doubt to hold me up to a good light. Amusing stories! How fun I was! How easygoing and irresistible was I?

What I didn't know was that Harrison may have been listening to me. To what I said. Specifically, about men. Listening for anything confirming that I was an available and experienced gal! He could have been gathering these rosebuds in order to come to the conclusion that he might have wanted to come to. Or, the one he ultimately came to anyway. The conclusion that it would be okay to take me home with him, or take me to my house with him. And that was that.

All through the *Star Wars* workweek I waited in vain for some indication that (a) we had ever been together at all (or had I imagined the entire event?) and/or (b) if indeed it *had* occurred, would it ever occur again in any form, ranging from another inarticulate weekend to finally marrying (after a discreet amount of time had elapsed since his eventual and uncomplicated divorce). I'm sure that on our relative lists of priorities as we went about filming, I might have ranked as high as number fifteen on his agenda, while Harrison was my number one. So this was the way I made it from that first weekend to that second. Would we share another monosyllabic weekend, or would I spend the ensuing Saturday and Sunday virtually alone, wondering what I'd done to already push him away? How could I have when we had barely been that close, just close enough to ignite an almost full-on obsession in me?

But spend a second weekend we did. Once again we were together in our apart way. We met at the North Star Pub in St. John's Wood, between Elstree and central London.

I'm sure I selected the place because it was the pub I had gone to when I was at drama college all those months ago. Months from when I'd dropped out of drama college in order to star in a space fantasy called *Star Wars*. Which must've seemed like decades before that evening at the North Star, because essentially everything in my life had changed. I was no longer a drama student doing Shakespeare and Ibsen with a fellow-student boyfriend; I was now an actual actress with a job in a film that took place in a galaxy far, far away. A space fantasy. Perfect. And now I was having an affair with my costar from that film. Just like I pretended to want, without understanding what that meant, and here I was in a pub in London having a drink with him after a day of filming.

I believe I may have previously mentioned that Harrison was not a garrulous person. Given that, as we sat in the public house, I inadvertently held my breath quite a bit—a lot—while fretting over what I would and would not say during that evening. I knew without believing it that I would not say a charmingly helluva lot. I would be calm and succinct and ask thoughtful questions and then listen to his answers intently. Had I been able to manifest the demeanor just described, this would have been the night he discovered yet another of my many characteristics that would cause him to rethink any less than positive opinions he had—obviously prematurely—formed.

He would wonder where I had been all his life and then recall with a bemused, ironic sinking feeling that I had yet to be born for much of it. The important thing was that at least he'd met me now. He would remind himself to try to make up for all of our lost time for the rest of our compatible lives. But for now we didn't think about ever needing to make up for anything, as we had barely amassed any amount of time together at all.

In fact, what happened was Harrison and I both began to drink and at some point early on I said, "Do you want to see me do an imitation of you?"

Harrison didn't really walk, he swaggered, moving a bit like John Wayne in slow motion—he would take his seemingly bad attitude for a walk. In order to depict this, I moved out of sight around the corner from Harrison and after a moment reappeared, strolling as he strolled, sauntering my way into whatever fresh hell I found myself in. I'd become him, disenchanted Lord Ford, master of all he surveyed, if he got around to it. I studied my environment with bored disenchanted eyes and smirking mouth, behaving as if wherever I'd inadvertently found myself was no doubt some pathetic watering hellhole for a bunch of needy poseurs and poseur wannabes who unfortunately didn't have the stuff to interest me/him.

I hadn't looked at Harrison yet to see how my portrayal of him was going over—too busy appearing indifferent and impatient with my surroundings. I'd get around to him in good time. Until then, what criminally inept person had decorated this room I was in? Decorated? More like defiled! Wow. I was amazed my eyes weren't bleeding from the insult some referred to as interior—shouldn't that be *inferior*?—decoration.

As I continued to portray his inner monologue as I imagined it, I finally let at least one of my eyes slide wearily over to his face and saw that he was not only laughing, he was laughing that silent and hard laugh reserved for true enthusiasm. Almost forty years later, I still think of it as one of the greater moments of my life. My "love" life.

I tried not to let my relief interrupt my imitation and returned my gaze to the disenchanting room around us, but I didn't intend for my portrayal to go on much longer—why press my luck? I mean, this could really be a game changer. If my portrait of my costar as a smug, scruffy-looking nerf herder went well enough, Harrison could unexpectedly (but gently and responsibly) leave his wife, and after a barely noticeable, dignified amount of time, he would marry me (in an unsentimental, tasteful way) and we would subsequently astonish everyone—including ourselves—by remaining together for the rest of whoever died first's life. And all because I dared to do an imitation of him, for him, in the pub one night! That was the beginning of his realizing that I was the only person with whom he felt comfortable enough to be . . . well, still uncomfortable, but now at peace with finding the world a constant disappointment. I continued to swagger toward him, and then next to him, finally letting my eyes return to him.

To my amazement I now saw that he was *still* laughing, which almost caused me to laugh, but instead I was able to maintain my portrayal, stretching my lips to their side limits to indicate what perhaps might be identified as a smile, but what turned out to be a cease between scowls before returning my expression to its relaxed smirk mode. I remember distinctly that this was the part of my impression that amused him the most.

Not that anything could convince me that our little dalliance was much more than that. A summer romance without the romance—or without the summer for that matter. Now that I had elicited this amazingly enthusiastic response from him, the danger was that I would want to get him laughing like a human during *all* our upcoming evenings together. It was bad enough that I was doing it already tonight. Please, God, don't let me feel the need to encourage him to be Mr. Chuckles on the set as well.

That would be a great idea, right? Making it my life's work to cause Han Solo to giggle his way through an asteroid field or howl with laughter at how ridiculously hairy his Wookie copilot was. How about a spit take in full view of some unobtrusive mynocks?

No, Harrison was not on this earth for me to goad into uncontrollable fits of laughter. I would have to control the impulse to entertain him, most importantly so as not to call attention to the possibility that we were more than just costars. Maybe not *much* more where he was concerned, but I was not so lucky.

Ah, men.

If I'd never succeeded in coaxing this coveted laughter of his out into the waiting world, I would never have known what I was missing—just that I was missing something, besides his not being single or accessible or, for the most part, warm. I wouldn't have been able to imagine his laughing wholeheartedly, or known how amazing it felt to actually be with the person you were with *and* feel that he liked you! You know, in that ongoing, let's-keep-seeing-each-other way.

This was the first time I felt as though Harrison liked me. Not because he wanted to sleep with me, or because no one else was around in a way that was convenient. He liked me. I'd made him laugh. I'd done an imitation of him, for him, even though I was afraid of how he'd react, and it had worked out! Take a risk, win a prize—or borrow someone else's prize for the duration of the film and hope things aren't too awkward when you film the sequels.

When he'd returned to his paranormal self, we sat smiling at each other, each waiting for the other to—what? Say something! Say something!

"I do other imitations," I finally offered, my shoulders up to my ears in a shrug. "But I don't think they'd go too well in this particular environment."

He lit a new cigarette and I quickly retrieved one of mine, letting him light it with another match while avoiding his eyes.

I went on. "Judy Garland for one—but you probably wouldn't like it."

"Why?"

"It's pretty loud and includes some dancing and a lot of makeup."

He nodded, picking some nicotine off the tip of his tongue and flicking it away. "Any more quiet ones? Like mine?"

I thought for a moment, searching for a funny reply. What to say? Make him laugh! Make him like me! Oh, please make him like me! Then everything will be fine or thereabouts. But no punch lines came to deliver that body blow that would reignite the blaze of his smile. What a jerk I was. I've always been a jerk and always will be. He hates me now and thinks I'm boring and stupid. B & S.

"I could do an imitation of my college boyfriend. He was super quiet." "Super"?! Who says "super" and lives? Certainly not me.

Harrison raised his eyebrows slightly. "Oh?"

"Yeah, well, maybe all boyfriends are quiet." Not boyfriends! Harrison wasn't my boyfriend and would never be. Fix this!

"Well, I wouldn't know about all boyfriends really," I rattled on. "Simon's really the first boyfriend I ever had. And I don't really—I'm not actually looking to—"

Harrison's face had whitened and his eyes were suddenly concerned. A slight frown threatened. "What do you mean, your *only* boyfriend?"

I blinked. What had I done now? I struggled for something to say.

"What about all those guys you talked about?" he asked. "That Rob guy—the photographer—and Fred and Buck and…"

Still frowning, I said, "Fred? I didn't sleep with him, I know him. Hey, you know him, too! Does that mean that *you* slept with him?"

Not waiting for a response, I continued, somewhat indignantly, "I don't sleep with all the men I know and I don't sleep with them just because I bring them up in conversation! Christ, if you thought that I slept with every man who found himself in some story of mine, you must think that I'm like a hooker or something! A slut! So I guess that made it all right for you!"

"Made what all right?"

"To fuck hookers! Your big, slutty costar... me!"

He interrupted, "All right! Enough!"

"Fine," I said, totally sulking, "but you shut up also."

(A version of that happened. A much toned-down version, maybe with fewer words and a lot less volume.)

Harrison was looking at the rug on the floor in front of him, blinking. Why was he so upset? Why did he want me to have slept with everyone with a penis that I brought up in conversation? He seemed so disappointed that I was as inexperienced as I'd suddenly revealed myself to be that I considered confessing that I'd let Buck feel me up under my shirt after the *Shampoo* wrap party (and then felt like a slut for days), but instead kept silent and watched the side of his suddenly serious face for clues as to why it was a bad idea that I'd only really been with him and Simon (oh, okay, and I'd slept with Griffin once in Las Vegas, but that didn't count because he was a friend and we never did it again).

I thought men liked it if you were inexperienced. Was

that only in Victorian times? Hadn't I once heard that some men even paid to deflower a girl—not that Harrison had deflowered me in any way (as though you could deflower someone a little). If so, was I then implying that he had maybe batted away a petal in the deflowering process? What was I meant to do here? How could I return him to the laughing Harrison from just moments ago—a time that, in the ensuing confusion, was now rapidly beginning to feel like weeks ago? Would he ever completely forgive me for not being sexually . . . what? Sophisticated? Experienced? For being a nineteen-year-old who, despite using four-letter words with such ease and familiarity, didn't turn out to be the pro, Scarlet Woman, tramp nymphomaniac I seemed to be?

It didn't occur to me until decades later that perhaps what disturbed Harrison was the implication that he was subsequently burdened with something very like responsibility, in that he had somehow been given a gift he hadn't wanted or expected.

Well, we all know what happened after that . . . we slowly fell deeper and deeper in love (he more than I for obvious reasons). It was truly a surprise to us both, the night he took my hand in his and weepingly admitted that though he loved his wife very much, they had been growing apart for quite some time now, so that when he met me he knew I was the person he wanted to spend the rest of his life with, both public and private. I was his soul mate—understanding him in ways he never thought possible. Here he had to stop speaking, he was crying so much, tears streaming down his manly face. Blowing his nose into his hand and wiping it on his shirt, he whispered, "Fate brought us together in space, but we brought ourselves together on Earth. But whether on Saturn or in South Kensington—please do me the honor of being the companion I share my life with." That was when he slipped the ring on my finger that I never take off except when I'm waxing my knuckles. A gold band with diamonds spelling out the word he came up with, "Carrison." (We also use it as a gate code in the home we share in London—in St. John's Wood near the North Star Pub, so we'll always be within walking distance of that place where we first discovered the shared passion that would continue secretly throughout our ongoing, enviable lives.)

How can I paint for you the picture of this brief three-month break in the bad weather of no feeling? Sadly, I cannot. And this is not because of the memory loss that typically comes with age—though that is a distinct factor. It is the memory loss that comes with marijuana use.

Though in this case, it is not the long-term use that has deprived me of the recollections from these months from long ago. It is the three-month ingestion of what seemed to me to be the brutal strength of Harrison's preferred strain of pot. This is what takes any and all vivid recollections and crushes them beneath its cruel inhaled heel.

At the time, the reefer took whatever certainty I possessed while in Harrison's company and traded it for paranoia so intense it took my breath away. What I recall from the rubble of my brain cells is the discomfort I experienced between waking and sleeping, trying to think of something to say other than "Do you love me?" or "Why are you with me at all?" or "Do you know your lines for next week?" or "Can I get you another beer?" or "Where did you get that scar on your chin?" By the way, I believe the answer to that question had the words "acid" and "girl with freckles" in it, and "the toilet seat hit my head and cracked this cut into my chin." But I am more than probably wrong.

I also doubt much of this was actually said per se, but I know he lay on his back on the couch in Riggs's apartment telling me the story. And if he did say any of it, I'm sure he made it up.

Though there has been some speculation regarding my drug use during *Star Wars*, I used nothing other than Harrison's pot on the weekends during that first film. After that, marijuana was no longer possible for me—it had such a powerful, all-consuming effect on me that I have never used that drug again.

In effect, I can't remember now what I was too uncomfortable to remember at the time. For three months. From celebration to intoxication to assignation to infatuation to imitation to indignation—this was my trimester of the affair that was Carrison.

Harrison finished shooting first. My last scenes would be two weeks later, so I decided to go back to L.A. for a break and wound up flying there with Harrison. I wasn't in charge of the movie's travel arrangements, so I couldn't have organized things so that he and I sat together, but sit together we did, for a full fourteen hours. In coach.

I don't know if he was pleased with these arrangements, because he didn't exhibit emotions and I didn't record it in the journals I kept, but we did wind up talking. Anyway, whatever I don't remember of our conversation on the flight, I do remember that he was kind. Kind enough to enable me to close the door on our cinematic episode together, both on- and offscreen, without regret. Which was quite a turn of events when you consider all those silent weekends.

"I'm a hick," I recall saying to him.

"No," Harrison answered. "You think you're less than

you are. You're a smart hick." And then, "You have the eyes of a doe and the balls of a samurai."

It's the only thing he ever said to me that acknowledged any intimacy between us, and it was enough. Not only because it had to be, but because of what I'm assuming it cost him to go that out of character in conversation. We never again acknowledged that anything of that nature had occurred.

Anyway, I keep mentioning these diaries. The ones I kept during the filming of the first *Star Wars*, the diaries I had forgotten about but recently found. By now, you're all ears. Or eyes. Time for the reveal.

judgemen
abulary
each other
indicating som
were unwillin
to articulate

just for y
you knew all along
foolish and worthless
were, you just hoped
if you crouched down
and yourself enough
wouldn't see it. But
day when your gua
is off duty you see the
you both catch
at yourself. catch
behaving. And t
No. You
Better c

notes from his periphery, or the glib martyr

One could never call me a quitter
I take something right and see it
Through till it's wrong
Auctioning myself off to the lowest bidder
Going once, going twice
Gone
Sold to the man for the price of disdain
Some are sold for a song
I don't rate a refrain.

I guess it was all going just a little too well
If I wasn't careful I'd be happy pretty soon
Heaven's no place for one who thrives on hell,
One who prefers the bit to the silver spoon.
Then just when I'd almost resigned myself to winning
When it seemed my bright future would never dim
When my luck looked as though it was only beginning
I met him.

. . .

Sullen and scornful; a real Marlboro man
The type who pours out the beer and eats
the can
A tall guy with a cultivated leer
One you can count on to disapprove or
disappear
I knew right away that he was a find
He knew that you had to be cruel to be kind
Given this, he was the kindest man I'd ever met
Back came my sense of worthlessness
And my long lost pangs of regret
I was my old self again, lost and confused
Reunited with that old feeling
Of being misunderstood and misused.

Sold to the man for the price of disdain
All of this would be interesting
If it weren't so mundane.

He is like a fantasy. The inevitability of his escape is most likely his most attractive feature. He submits to the silences without a struggle; I go under shrugging and sighing, finally overcome by the sheer weight of the pause-turned-lull-turned-way-of-life. Silence speaks louder than words—it screams, "BORING!" He's boring and tries to make it look more like a decision than an accident. The silences make my composure decompose from the inside out.

I wonder what he is like inside out. We often assume that when the surface offers so little the depth must be unfathomable. Whatever is inaccessible must be worthwhile. I hate him and all of his quiet. But I love the implied disapproval, the seniority, the sternness, the disdain, the "strong silent type."

Frightening awful silences. Hiding behind all those mannerisms and quiet, crouched down behind himself. Unfiltered cigarettes, beer, broads and lumberjack shirts. And all that quiet to read into. One not only has to read between the lines, one has to fill him in altogether. Because he's not there. To make him important in one's life requires an overactive imagination. Unfortunately, mine never knows when to quit.

During the long stretches of silence one can study him, eventually filling him in to suit one's likes or dislikes. (The satisfaction of one's fantasy.) I have filled him in to be unobtainable, disinterested, attractive and bored with my company. My ideal mate. Someone to endure, never to enjoy. I am totally at his mercy. I suffer through the silence, imagining that he is suffering my company. That I am merely an alternative for nothing better to do. I'm frightened of the power I have given him over me and of how he will almost certainly abuse it, merely by not being fully aware he has it.

So he assumes his apathetic poker face and I sit practicing wry knowing looks somewhere in his periphery. I don't dare pick a topic for fear that it won't be funny enough or interesting enough for his awe-inspiring judgment. With his silence he establishes himself as a sort of trapped audience and so you break your ass to meet the enormous challenge of entertaining him, frantic with worry that his teeth might suffocate. Oh, he's very funny sometimes with his parched sense of humor. But he only plays himself part-time. I work myself around the clock—obviously I have not heard about the child labor laws. But then

I have not totally accepted that I am no longer a child. Once I do that I will have to accept responsibility for everything I do.

We have no feeling for one another. We lie buried together during the night and haunt each other by day. Acting out something that we don't feel and seeing through something that doesn't deserve any focus. I have never done anything quite like this.

I sit patiently awaiting the consequences. I talk, walk, eat and sleep patiently awaiting the consequences. How can a thing that doesn't seem to be happening come to an end? George says that if you look at the person someone chooses to have "a relationship" with, you'll see what they think of themselves. So Harrison is what I think of myself. It's hardly a relationship, but nevertheless he is a choice. I examined all the options and chose the most likely to leave. No emotional investments. Never love for me—only obsession. Someone has to stand still for you to love them—my choices are always on the run.

I can't think about it anymore. It makes my head hurt. My mind works overtime trying to rationalize it, categorize it, define it until it no longer means anything. Put it into words—you can't feel words. I think that if I could give a name to what I feel it would go away. Find the word that describes the feeling and say it over and over until it's merely a sound.

That old familiar feeling of hopelessness. That vague sense of desperation; fighting not to lose something before you've decided what you've got. I must thank him someday for teaching me to be casual. I realize I'm not very adept at it yet, but given a certain amount of time I feel I could learn to act as though I wanted to be somewhere else, maybe even manage to look as though I *was* somewhere else. I can charm the birds out of everybody else's trees but his. Vultures are difficult to charm unless you're off somewhere rotting in the noonday sun. Casually rotting... a glib cadaver.

I'm sorry it's not Mark—it could've been. It should've been. It might've meant something. Maybe not much, but certainly more.

This is a totally unreal situation but it's the only reality I've got. I call friends trying to recapture some of my old dime-store perspective, but no matter how long we talk or how deep we delve I can't seem to make any of it stick. I don't really know how any of this feels. It's important to decide whether all this is right or wrong, but as I've always seemed to judge myself in terms of other people's standards and opinions; I have no moral reserves of my own to tap. I've always relied on the kindness of strangers, acquaintances, friends, relatives and Tennessee Williams to see me through. I'm quite sure, though, that if I had any principles what I'm doing now would violate most all of them.

I suspect that no matter what happens I will allow it to hurt me. Eat away at my insides, as it were—as it will be. As it always has been. Why am I so accessible? Why do I give myself to people who will always and should always remain strangers? I have always relied on the cruelty of strangers and I must stop it now. I am a fool. I need a vacation from myself. I'm not very good at it lately.

Who do you want them to think you are? How do you think people see you? Or don't you let them near enough to see. You make up their minds for them. Do you think that you succeed in convincing people that you are what you seem to be? You make people meet you on your own territory. You don't help them. You let them verbally hang themselves and then feel better about yourself, your power, your own sense of worth. You have the power to alienate them and if they allow it, you might even manage to make them feel awkward and foolish—foolish for letting you affect them at all. Do you want them to like you? Or are you one of those people who "don't care what people think." You're not living your life for them, so why should you give a fuck what people think? You make people come to you and, when they eventually do, you punish them with your smugness. Nothing ever out of character.

I wish you would love me more so that I could love you less.

—Not Me

The man sitting alone so silent and strong
So what if you're attracted for all the wrong reasons
So what if your reasoning's wrong
Call his indifference mystery
Call his arrogance intellect
All you've got to lose is your heart
And a little self-respect.
If you've got arrogance and indifference
You can make them pay
They're the most commercial product
On the romantic market today.

What do you think I feel for you or think of you? How sophisticated do you think I am? That's not a fair question because obviously I don't even know how to answer it. I overestimated myself. I thought I could be with the big kids. The grown-ups. The ones who ask questions like they already know the answers. Who never give themselves away; no emotional souvenirs.

What's happening to me? Who the hell do I think I am? Why have I become casually involved with someone who, if I am totally honest with myself, I don't care for and who doesn't care for me? And is married?

I must figure this thing out once and for all—this pattern of becoming obsessed with inaccessible men. I think I've just about covered the boards by now. I think I've bled it dry. First homosexual men, already established in their inaccessibility before I came along, so I couldn't take it too personally—just personally enough to get the taste in my mouth. The taste of disinterest and abandonment, sort of like cottage cheese with an aftertaste similar to smoked haddock. From then on it seemed I couldn't get enough. As it were—as it seems to be. I started with snacking on the inaccessibility of random silent jerks and seem to have arrived at making a full meal of it. Now I've had more than enough. I want the check. Waiter?

Thanks for the good times. Thank you for being so generous with what you have withheld. Thank you for being the snake in my grass, the thorn in my side, the pain in my ass, the knife in my back, the wrench in my works, the fly in my ointment. My Achilles' heart. Caught in a whirlpool without an anchor, relaxing into it, calmly going under for one of many last times.

I've got to learn something from my mistakes instead of establishing a new record to break. Maybe stop fooling around with all these human beings and fall in love with a chair. It would have everything that the immediate situation has to offer, and less, which is obviously what I need. Less emotional and intellectual feedback, less warmth, less approval, less patience and less response. The less the merrier.

Chairs. They're always there when you need them and, while their staying implies total devotion, they still manage to remain aloof, noncommittal and insensitive. Immovable and loyal. Reliable and unconsoling. Chairs it is. I must furnish my heart with feelings for furniture.

But with these human beings you never know. They might not want to hurt you. They might even like you, and that would be the worst possible thing that could happen. Because what can you do with people that like you, except, of course, inevitably disappoint them?

It's very dangerous to have someone like you, because one day he'll find that you are not the person he thought you were. He'll end up someday having only one thing in common with you and that'll be a shared sense of contempt and disgust for you. Of course you knew all along how foolish and worthless you were, you just hoped that if you crouched down behind yourself enough he wouldn't see it. But one day when your guard is off-duty you see him see. You both catch you at yourself. Catch you behaving. And then you're lost. No. You were lost all along.

Don't offer me love
I seek disinterest and denial
Tenderness makes my skin crawl
Understanding is vile
When you offer me happiness
You offer too much
My ideal is a long-lasting longing
For someone whom I cannot quite touch

I am the only one who can come to my rescue. I am the only one who can help me now. But I don't know how to help myself. It must follow then that I don't want to help myself. That I want to completely drain myself of all hope, which will leave me safe and dry with nothing to lose. The point where it can only get better, if I allowed it to get better.

I can't focus on the good things. There are good things going on all around me, but I don't trust them, I can't make use of them, don't have the time for them; I'm too preoccupied with my precious panic. It seems to be demanding almost all of my attention. My own personal private collection of panic.

I need to write. It keeps me focused for long enough to complete thoughts. To let each train of thought run to its conclusion and let a new one begin. It keeps me thinking. I'm afraid that if I stop writing I'll stop thinking and start feeling. I can't concentrate when I'm feeling. I try to put the feelings into thoughts or words but it always seems to come out in disjointed sweeping statements. Adolescent jargon peppered with random selections from a fairly gaudy vocabulary. A Frederick's of Hollywood vocabulary. I wish that I could leave myself alone. I wish that I could finally feel that I punished myself enough. That I deserved time off for all my bad behavior. Let myself off the hook, drag myself off the rack where I am both torturer and torturee.

I confide in everyone. I have no restricted private self, reserved specifically for certain trusted special people. I trust and mistrust anyone. I have traveled a full circle. But this time, on returning to zero again, I am able to act out the mistake more adeptly. I am on my way to becoming a very skilled loser. A specialist, a loser to end all losers. A flair for failing. I do it with style and finesse.

I'm on physical and mental reserves. Carefully selecting and gathering all the ingredients for my recipe for ruin. Homemade hysteria. Fresh from my mind and ready to serve. Torment to go. I must never again involve myself in a situation that makes me feel this sordid.

Hand over hand on the way to the top
So afraid to fall back to the beginning
Wishing it were more of a drop

Happiness beckons you
In the guise of money and fame
It can all be yours someday
At the drop of a name

To be one of the familiar faces
Calling the shots on a first-name basis
That's your desire
But you've got to get a lot higher
On the ladder
Then nothing will matter
You'll be all set
On top of the world
That's where you want to get

A household word
Like Ajax or Abbe Lane
A reputation to live up to

An explosion to sustain
Watch him! There he goes, folks, higher and
higher
Hoping to get out of the anonymous frying pan
And into the Hollywood fire

The compromise I made was not an easy thing to do
It was either you or me and I chose you
Although far from a joker you spoke in wry, wry riddles
I could've given you so much but you wanted so little
I thought you might supply some tenderness I lacked
But out of all the things I offered you took my breath away
And now I want it back

I never had what I wanted because I would never want what I had
I thought you were different, prettier than most and twice as bad
Uncompromising and caustic, sort of short and sometimes sweet
I tried to read between your lines as you would so rarely speak
But I gave you far more credit than you were actually due

You see I thought I was only seeing half the man
But that was all there was to you

You took my breath away
Took my breath away
You took my breath away
And now I want it back

I am closer to who I want to be when I am alone lately. With people, I hear my voice and I just wonder who or what I'm doing all this for. Spreading myself out in front of people. Devaluing my ostensible worth by being so readily available to almost any random pedestrian who wanders into the crosswalk of my focus. If someone is within an earshot I shoot off at the mouth.

This drug has placed me in the eye of the hurricane. Or is it a tornado? Whatever it is, it's a whole lot of weather, placing everything valuable in jeopardy. If I could only get a fixed idea myself, I wouldn't have to constantly look to other people. Trying to outguess them, to convince them of my idea of myself. Hoping that if they believe that's who I am, then maybe I'll be able to believe it, too. But when they do believe it, when they seem convinced that I am who I'm seeming to be—and they even approve—I inevitably feel that I've fooled them. That they must be pretty goddamn gullible to fall for my routines.

My panic is rising again. My sense of isolation and worthlessness. And no other senses worth mentioning apparently. It's not nice being inside my head. It's a nice place to visit but I don't want to live in here. It's too crowded; too many traps and pitfalls. I'm tired of it. The same old person, day in and day out. I'd like to try something else. I tried to neaten my mind, file everything away into tidy little thoughts, but it only got more and more cluttered. My mind has a mind of its own. I try to define my limits by seeing just how far I can go, and I find that I passed them weeks ago. And I've got to find my way back.

Stop playing the part of the glib martyr. You're just trying to make cyanide out of 7-Up. I talk about myself in the third person, as if I were talking about a child of mine, or a new television series. I talk about myself behind my back. I talk about my private life and self like they were just common gossip. I make and sell myself cheap. I serialize myself. I am the *Mad* magazine version of *Psychology Today*. I waste myself.

Here's what he said: People adapt to you. Don't worry, you can't alter what they think of you to any great degree, and by the same token what they think of you can't alter you. You sit patiently, awaiting that dreaded yet hoped-for disapproval. You're afraid you seem foolish or pretentious. You pounce on everything you say with a pair of tweezers and pluck it about until you can't remember exactly what it is you said, what context it was in, if you even said it, and if anyone heard you at all. And how much their opinion means to you. Are their mental credentials so impressive that you have to put yourself behind their eyes, find yourself loathsome and/or boring, and then make it matter?

Why am I in such a hurry to find out what people think of me? I even have gone to the trouble of playing myself broadly in order to hurry up their decision. I give them one of many varieties of brief or not-so-brief summaries from which they can draw a conclusion. It depends on how much time and energy I've got and then I give away portions of myself according to that. I mustn't allow myself to get sucked into thinking that it's romantic to be neurotic, that being neurotic means one has to be complicated and somewhat intellectual. Deep. Proud of the fact that you can sink to the depths of despair. A neurotic, complicated, somewhat intellectual, deep gal who's also wacky, zany and madcap. A must at a wake.

I must be who I am and people adjust to it. Don't try to rush or influence the decision. Do not let what you think they think of you make you stop and question everything you are. Surely between the various yous, you can find that you not only have enough going for you to keep you going, but to "take you far." Maybe even to Alderaan and back.

Who are you doing all this bullshit for? Certainly not yourself. If you were the only one around to be yourself for, you'd stop for the lack of interest. You know all the shit you tell people—you know it, you've lived it, you're living it, etc. So what's the point of telling any and everybody else? Ingratiating yourself to them by being so available. "Admitting" and "confessing" and "confiding" all those things that sound secret and special and spontaneous when it's really just the same old ploy. Seduction. I would resent if I were on the outside looking in. Someone telling me things I didn't ask to hear. Telling me things I don't want to hear. Too much, too soon, and I don't know what she wants in return. Am I supposed to nod and smile, look interested, or does she expect me to exchange stories? Does she expect me to tell her about my childhood, my parents, guilt, anxiety, fears, sexuality? 'Cause if she does she's got another thing coming.

I should let people I meet do the work of piecing me together until they can complete, or mostly complete, the puzzle. And when they're finished they can look at the picture that they've managed to piece together and decide whether they like it or not. On their own time. Let them discover you.

You're my thought collector
Part-time love rejector
Draggin' round and round and round in my
dreams
And you make me smile
Decorate my meanwhile
Drivin' me to extremes
Can you hear me, my sweet chauffeur
Drivin' me to extremes

Something really incredible happened to me. Something that should've happened a long time ago, but Jesus, I'm just grateful it happened. I mean, it's changed everything. You're probably thinking, oh, she's falling in love, or she's found God, or the IRA, or whatever. But it's nothing like that. Although in a way it's like all of those things because it's a kind of revolutionary deep emotional religious experience. And yet not like that at all. I suppose I should just tell you exactly what happened and let it speak for itself.

I was sitting by myself the other night doing the usual things one does when spending time alone with yourselves. You know, making mountains out of molehills, hiking up to the top of the mountains, having a Hostess Twinkie and then throwing myself off the mountain. Stuff like that. Anyway, I'd done this... oh, 4, maybe 5... we'll call it an even 19 times. I was just about ready to start construction on my 20th molehill when I suddenly thought I heard someone playing a polka outside my window.

I later discovered that it was a recording of Ray Conniff jamming live at the Troubadour with Led

Zeppelin. It was early Ray Conniff, before he got really commercial. When he was still really mellow and innovative and . . . Well, when his music got <u>inside</u> you, you know what I mean? You remember the days when everyone would rush home from school, grab some Fritos and Ripple wine, put on their favorite Ray Conniff album and just unwind. And finding out when his new album was coming out and rushing down to Discount Records, hoping that they've not sold out.

I know one guy who actually saw a Ray Conniff concert, before he stopped giving them because the girls would scream so loud that you couldn't hear his music. But this guy was close and could hear pretty well and he was just... Well, completely blown away. I mean, he said it was so fucking moving, you know? He said that Ray Conniff, and I do not make this up, he said that Ray Conniff was the most real person, the most together person, he'd ever seen. And this guy's been around and met them all—yes, including Mantovani—and yet Ray Conniff was the one person whose mere presence and even merer music moved him profoundly.

Anyway, all this has nothing to do with my experience really, except I think it is somehow ironic that

I should be sitting there and suddenly hear this incredible music that had meant so much to me. So I stopped work on my molehill and went to the window to see where this music was coming from. Suddenly I noticed a light in the distance that seemed to be coming towards me. As it grew closer I could see the light was coming from a fire. I look back on this and find it really strange and sort of eerie, but at the time I thought nothing of it. It was almost 5 feet in front of me when I realized I was looking at a man sitting on a flaming pie. He smiled serenely at me—or maybe he coughed violently—but whatever it was, it was mystical. Almost embarrassingly mystical, if you know what I mean.

The man must have noticed me blushing because he offered me a rainbow trout and enough money to finish my payments on my new Dyna-Gym. My eyes filled with tears and he leaned over and wiped my eyes with the trout and then said, "You needn't ever make mountains out of molehills again. You have misjudged yourself. You are not who you think you are. You have been examining yourself from the wrong end of the telescope, one might say. You can set up housekeeping on one side of the looking glass or the other—the side that makes big things small or small things big; I like to hang out on the big things small side, you meet a better class of people there. But of late, you haven't been able to see yourself clearly. You see, my dear, you are not Carrie Fisher at all. They just told you that to test you. Well, now, my dear, the test is over, and I'm pleased to say you pass with a C–. Now you can graduate to your true identity. You see, my dear, you are really Mr. Ed. And you have been all along. You can now live out your life as who you were intended to be. Farewell."

As I watched him disappear on his flaming pie, I suddenly noticed the rainbow trout smiling at me from the windowsill where the mystical pie man had left him. I started to ask if I could get him something—a drink, or some bait—when he suddenly let out a shrill laugh, as only a fish can do. I politely asked him what was so funny and he said, "You. So you're Mr. Ed. Old horse face with the dumb jokes. No wonder you got canceled." Then he laughed again and continued laughing until he fell off the windowsill and into the street below.

He lay in the street the entire night screaming with laughter and then suddenly the laughing stopped. I don't know what happened to him. Although recently someone was talking about the sequel Don Knotts was doing to The Incredible Mr. Limpet (The Incredible Mr. Limpet Two) and they were describing the fish that had the lead opposite Knotts, and it could only have been my rainbow trout.

Mystical, huh?

There are plenty of fish in the sea
And you sure look like a fish to me
As soft as a crayfish with a mouth that opens
and closes
And like a fish you don't say pretty things
And you don't send no roses
There are plenty of fish in plenty of seas
And like a fish you don't bring shiny diamonds
And fall to your knees

If you'd never gotten close I wouldn't have
noticed when you were far away
But you filled up my nights and then emptied
my days
There are girls who can be helped and there are
girls who can be had
But you helped me and then had me
And now fish I need help again I need help
real bad

. . .

But, like the fisherman said, there are plenty of fish in the sea
And maybe someday some sweet salmon will come and swim away with me

When we talk it's not merely idle chatter
We discuss things that really don't matter
We talk of love and god and pain
To life's never-ending song
We add yet one more refrain
And as the pace gets more and more frantic
The words get more and more pedantic
We leave no sophistry unturned
As our rhetoric becomes more intense
Using our very large vocabularies
To disguise our very common sense.

The words get longer and the plot gets thinner
Another discourse to discuss at dinner
There is no feeling we can't analyze
Seizing each chance to intellectualize
Talking in the past and present tense
We're making a lot more noise
And a lot less sense.

She: I love you.

He: What?

She: Nothing... never mind.

[Pause]

He: Is something the matter? I mean, you seem sort of uncomfortable.

She: Me?... No, I'm fine... I feel like a water lily floating on a Chinese lagoon.

He: You what?

She: I said, I feel like a... Oh, never mind! Everything's fine—I'm fine.

He: You sure?

She: Yes.... I'm just a little wired that's all.

He: You want anything?

She: Anything.

He looks at her for a moment then stares off into space nodding.

She laughs.

He: What?

She: Mmm?

He: You looked like you were about to say something.

She: Did I? I always look like that, I guess. It's kind of a twitch.

He looks off into space.

Sheila and Hugh

Resting in arms
Testing your charms
Repeating a ritualized "I love you"
Sharing a fight
Or a kiss in the night
Shrugging when friends ask "What's new?"

After the wedding
Her hips started spreading
His hair line began to recede
They remained together
Out of habit now
And not out of any great need

He'll show up from work
Showing signs of strain
While her day was spent cleaning
Letting the soap operas wash her brain

...

He reads the evening paper
She calls him in to eat
They share their meal silently
She's bored, he's just beat

Then they climb the stairs
Multiplying the monotony
With each step they take
The hours spent sleeping
They find more satisfying
Than those spent awake

He removes his work clothes
She puts on her curlers and cream
Hoping the sheets will protect them
From the demon of daily routine

Then he clicks off the lamp
And the darkness holds no noise
For in the dark you can be anyone
Housewives will be girls
And businessmen boys

. . .

"I love you, Sheila"
I love you, *Hugh"*
But she's deciding on dishes
And his thoughts are all askew

And the sheets supply refuge
For this perpetual pair
Neither really knowing anymore
Why the other one is there

I act like someone in a bomb shelter trying to raise everyone's spirits.

He's far from a fool, nowhere near. I'm quite near. I can feel the fool that's so far away from him breathing down my neck.

I would like to not be able to hear myself think. I constantly hear my mind chattering and jabbering away up there all by itself. I wish it would give me a fucking break. Write, don't think, write. You're not thinking properly, Ms. Fisher, I suggest you write.

If anyone reads this when I have passed to the big bad beyond I shall be posthumously embarrassed. I shall spend my entire afterlife blushing.

I'm scared. Scared that I'll let Harrison hurt me. That I'll change plain old leaving into abandonment again. It's no mean feat. Hurting might be familiar but it certainly isn't fun. It's a bit pathetic to set yourself up to be humiliated or passed over or whatever and then at the last minute deciding it really wasn't what you had in mind—perhaps you could show me something in rayon.

None of us have been really given the opportunity to explore the possibility that, given our own situation, we might not choose to see one another. We're thrown together and we make the best of one another if for no other reason than convenience. Would we still seek out each other's company in "REAL LIFE," when we regained our temporarily suspended perspective? I don't think we could honestly say at this point. We could very easily be deceived by the sheer convenience of one another and the seeming absence of options. At this point your main objective would be to find someone—anyone—as long as they were close, willing and this side of the grave. (It's not difficult to live up to those qualifications.) Something handy, immediate and as human as possible. We aren't really in the position to be choosy. The real test is being in a situation where it's not just convenient—where there are a substantial number of alternatives to the more than likely possibility of coming down with a case of 24-hour loneliness.

Anyway as George's wife Marcia says, we're gold in the same place (referring to the theory that we look for people that are gold in the place where we're shit and shit in the places where we're gold), so instead of picking up where you leave off, we pick up and leave off in practically the same place (that place being somewhere between high school and Gilligan's Island).

I do not want to take part in my life. It can just go on without me; I'm not giving it any help. I don't want to see it, I don't want to talk to it, I don't want it anywhere near me. It takes too much energy. I refuse to be a part of it. If you have a life, even if you get used to it ruining your sleep, spoiling your fun, requiring your somewhat undivided attention, what overwhelming relief one must feel when it finally skips town.

I don't like having to keep the spinning plates spinning on top of all their various and sun-dried poles. From now on they can fall off the poles and break for all I care. I censor myself and where the fuck does it get you? Gussying up your thoughts and putting them to paper.

A woman's place is in the home
Seated by the telephone
Men sow their wild oats
And women are sown

Here I am again
Making the same mistake
Instead of learning my lesson
I just establish a new record to break.

What's the riddle?
Me talking so much
And saying so little

She: One of us is boring.

He: Why do you say that?

She: Because . . . well, we're just sitting here, not talking.

He: What's wrong with that?

She: Well, I don't know. Probably nothing—it's just that we don't need each other for it.

He: For what?

She: Being quiet.

The itsy bitsy spidered his way up my water spout
He little Jack Hornered his way into my corner
And now I can't get him out
He ate all my porridge, sat in my chair
Slept in my bed, washed himself into my hair
Hey, all you king's horses!
Whether you're horse's asses or men,
Could you pretty please piece my heart
Back together again?

Love has made me what I am today
But as to what that is I really couldn't say
One thing's for certain
I am quite alone
Cause there are none so quiet
As those who will not phone
And there is no one as far past caring
As he who just don't care
I've washed that man right into my hair
He's sat in my chair and slept in my bed
He's eaten all my porridge and climbed inside my head

Maybe no man is an island
But some might as well be
The type whose bats
Always seem to get in your belfry

What am I getting myself into that I don't want out of?

I can't remember beginning, I can't conceive of ending. That I am afraid of, that I need, that I find unlike anything I could ever have imagined or anticipated, that I can't do without, that I don't know what to do with a cliché.

And what if I said I loved you? What then? To justify some delinquent desire with the confessions of some emotion? You'd know where you stood—right on my feet. It needn't be anything. But it's the possibility that leaves us delirious with dull discussions.

This is fairly new. Incurable optimist that I am, I am bravely inclined to think it's temporary. The hundred-dollar question: "What do we mean to one another?" Afraid the answers won't support each other. And all this talking around the issue. But what is it? "Let's define our relationship," you bastard. I spend my entire epic existence vacillating between extremes and I think possibly this might be changing—but no. What the fuck happened to the in-between? Midway between passive and panicked. I seem to become involved in situations that only allow for tension. I'm beginning to think, "Relaxation is a rumor, a vicious rumor started by a sadistic..."

We could come to a full stop now if you think that would help. Because like any other B-movie heroine, I can't go on like this. Can you understand? I don't want to hurt you any more than I want you to hurt me. It's now a question of surviving each other's company instead of enjoying it.

Trying relentlessly to make you love me, but I don't want the love—I quite prefer the quest for it. The challenge. I am always disappointed with someone who loves me—how perfect can he be if he can't see through me?

I can just get so close
Till I begin to suffocate
I must go back to the surface
To breathe
I catch my breath
I manage to breathe
Offhandedly supplying distance
While I seemingly never leave
To compensate
For my lack of honesty
I entertain with distorted truths
My inadequacies and obsessions—
If a personality can be promiscuous
Mine would be quite loose
Try as I might
I can give to you no more
Than I give the next person
Or the last
I set the stage by establishing positions
You are the audience
I—the cast
I try to be somewhat exclusive
Somehow I never quite succeed

We'll keep in touch

But enough

Is too much

I'll need new disinterest on which to feed

Of course I'm playing a losing hand
A hand on which I invite you to tread
If only I could love someone
But I've chosen to love
Anyone
Instead.

Hey check-coated guy
Blow your smoke into my favorite eye.
Steal your arm around me
Till you've finally found me.
All under a moonlit sky.
Oh my
All under a moonlit sky.
Moving side to side
On a dampening lawn
My head falling to his shoulder
He stifling a deep yawn.
The party fast receding
Leaving the dancers with the night
Someone runs some water
Someone turns out a light

Half woman and half bar stool
The room spinning round from rounds of drink
She sits hunched over her wine glass
Returning any time she was given to think

"Who am I doing it for," I asked him. It was a fairly rhetorical question and the only reply it warranted was a shrug, which he supplied. I sat on the floor engrossed in the empty space before me. He lay stretched out on the couch looking sturdy and sure. Maybe no man is an island, but some sure look like one. All safe and dry and looming on your horizon. But the current was against me and who was I kidding? His island was already inhabited and here I was, a teenaged trespasser. All I had to do was make the most of being adrift.

He yawned. I looked at him with a minimal amount of expectancy. He looked over at me, and I had to look away. I didn't want him to see that I "belonged to him"—it was bad enough that I knew it. I didn't want him to know it, too. I kept it from myself for almost 2 months now, calling it everything from "physical" to a big mistake. Not that it wasn't those things, it was, but when I "gave myself to him"—Merry Christmas, baby—I gave myself for a while, not just for a good time.

But whatever kind of time it was, it was running out. He was leaving Sunday. So there we were, Tuesday night sitting in the lurch that he would leave me in. Nothing personal, of course. He finished filming and had to go home to his wife and kids. Aye, there's the rub. That's when Cinderella's pre-shattered post-ball shoe was scheduled to drop.

With him love was easier done than said
Instead of taking you to heart he would take
you to bed
And you take what he has to offer lying down
You're getting more involved while he's still
getting around

It's all a matter of touch and go
Cause he's one for all and all for show
But after all was said and almost done
I was playing for keeps and he was playing
for fun

I call people sometimes hoping not only that they'll verify the fact that I'm alive but that they'll also, however indirectly, convince me that be ing alive is an appropriate state for me to be in. Because sometimes I don't think it's such a bright idea. Is it worth the trouble it takes trying to live life so that someday you get something worthwhile out of it, instead of it almost always taking worthwhile things out of you?

I wish I could go away somewhere but the only problem with that is that I'd have to go, too.

forty years on

How I've portrayed Harrison is how Harrison was with me forty years ago. I've gotten to know him a bit better over time, and as such somewhat differently. He's an extremely witty man and someone who seems more comfortable with others than he is, or ever was, with me. Maybe I make him nervous. Maybe I talk so much he can't get a word in edgewise. Maybe it's our mutual gestalt. Maybe I exasperate him. Probably a bit of all four.

But perhaps the most important reason, maybe, just maybe, we didn't speak much was because the subject of our relationship was off-limits. And that was the elephant herd in the room to tiptoe around. So we sat amongst the elephants and ignored them together. It was our biggest activity, the biggest thing that we shared other than *Star Wars* dialogue and the painfully obvious undiscussed.

My affair with Harrison was a very long one-night stand. I was relieved when it ended. I didn't approve of myself.

If Harrison was unable to see that I had feelings for him (at least five, but sometimes as many as seven) then he wasn't as smart as I thought he was—as I knew he was. So I loved him and he allowed it. That's as close a reckoning as I can muster four decades later.

I'm frequently still awkward in his presence, still struggle with what I'm going to say. I always imagine that he's thinking that I've just said something asinine, which may or may not be true.

And whatever was the state of his marriage, which ended soon after the filming of *Star Wars* for reasons having nothing whatsoever to do with me, I don't think of Harrison in any way as a "womanizer." I think he was lonely in England. We were all lonely in an upbeat beginning-of-our-public-lives way. I think. At least I was, and I'm making an educated guess about the others. None of us had ever starred in a movie before, and Harrison was the only one of an age where he could muster some perspective. We were on the Island of Location, and Location is the land of permission, where you can behave in ways that you would never behave in the real world.

There was Harrison and there was me. Both three months away from home. On location where you were free to do what neither of you would do when surrounded by your all-too-loving family and all-too-observant friends. Where everything and everyone around you was interesting and new. Where you have all sorts of new people now focused on you and how you are feeling. But not in the usual quasi-claustrophobic way. These were people who didn't want anything from you except that you have your lines memorized, your costume on, and your hair and makeup smooth and neat—especially your hair. Mine anyway, which tended to get unpinned and stray out of the confines it needed to stay in. Even though you were running around and shooting guns, your hair absolutely could not be in disarray. One had to look all neat and tidy while involved in the aerobic activity of saving the galaxy.

For most of us, home is an environment that discourages you from fooling around of any kind. Not that any of us were necessarily inclined to act out on adulterous impulses. I look back and see us all being playfully physical with one another, enjoying that familial comfort that developed amongst us. Us being me and Mark, though my focus on what happened between Mark and myself diminished once things began with Mr. Ford. On some days I would self-consciously draw back from contact with him, while on others I would have fun frolicking through brightly lit hallways, touching an arm, ducking down my bun-encased head, or grazing a powdered forehead to his smuggler's jacket, leaning over to look at some allegedly unremembered lines, falling into him, my smaller self to his larger one in a fit of suppressed laughter between takes. What's that saying I've said before? And I'll keep saying it until things can finally get unsaid? "Location, location, location."

Kissing me in the car was the last time that Harrison would be able to labor under the relaxing assumption that I was your average, everyday sexually experienced would-be actress. Someone accustomed to drunkenly jumping into the backs of cars and later falling into bed. A brief and amazingly casual encounter with said would-be actress, looking to add to her currently very short, but, like many other humans, over the ensuing years increasingly longer, line of exciting unclothed experiences with attractive men.

For me? A brief thrilling liaison I would eventually calmly walk away from, smiling and sophisticated. Anticipating the look on my friends' faces when I could safely and cavalierly recount that amusing tryst I'd had on this cool little sci-fi film I'd done in England. I would laugh ironically as I told my fascinated, impressed pals about this man whom I'd been attracted to—how could I not be, he was so handsome. I was barely old enough to vote but I could easily enlist in the army, and I enlisted into the army of him. But we'd both known from the start this wouldn't be a love affair, just two adult humans who hadn't fallen in love with each other but appreciated each other. We were both adults, why shouldn't we have had fun together! It never occurred to me to feel hurt because he hadn't fallen in love with me. It was better this way! Friendly feelings and wonderful sex—what a nice change it had been from my relationship with Simon in drama school—so emotional, so innocent and new. No mess, no fuss. There was him and there was me; none of your needy "couple" shit, right? And I was now five foot six inches tall, had green eyes, was slender, lithe, and free of self-pity all the time. Right. Sure.

But you've got to feel bad for Harrison (well, you don't *have* to, but if you can, for my sake, try). Not bad as in actually feeling a pang of anything emotional, gimme a break—no, just the sort of bad you might feel when someone is telling you a longish story about how they were talking about this surprise gift they bought for someone and then that someone overheard the conversation and the surprise was ruined. Oh no! How awful! What did you do? A ruined-surprise kind of awful, as opposed to, "Is that guy J.D. still living with you? Huh, because I was just at a drugstore and saw him picking up some medication and I overheard him tell the pharmacist it was for his leprosy." I mean there's bummer bad and then there's the "Oh my fucking shit! No way, you're kidding, right?" sort of bad. Blithely sympathetic bad or end-of-the-world bad. There, see? And all I was trying to do was say that I feel a little bad for Harrison at this point in my life (which he would loathe, so I take it back).

But when it was happening, I didn't feel bad for him; I only felt bad, and more than a little, for myself. Time shifts and your pity enables you to turn what was once, decades ago, an ordinary sort of pain or hurt, complicated by embarrassing self-pity, into what is now only a humiliating tale that you can share with others because, after almost four decades, it's all in the past and who gives a shit?

As I mentioned, a few times already, perhaps, en route between Elstree Studios and London, between Borehamwood and London, between surprise party and the next thing, Harrison and I spent quite a lot of time kissing. Later, Harrison informed me what a bad kisser I actually was then. Not that he knows (or anyone knows) what kind of a kisser I am—it's a secret. The remark would probably sting a bit even six thousand years after the event. But I wonder about it now. I wish I could return to Harrison—maybe while he was recuperating from some airplane accident or being crushed by a flying piece of film set. He would be lying in bed, a leg or two elevated, his brow smooth with forced serenity.

"Why did you think I was such a bad kisser?" I would ask casually.

He would look out the window at the failing lights, chewing the inside of his cheek quietly. Not that you can do that loudly without help.

"Maybe," I'd suddenly offer, "it was because I was so shocked to find myself on the receiving end of an offscreen kiss from some person I'd have an on-screen kiss with in a movie or two that my mouth just sort of hung open in amazement."

"Oh, shut up," he'd growl without looking at me. I always have him shut me up in our imagined interactions, probably because he always looks like he wants me to lose my grip on the English language.

Anyway, I suppose in part I'm telling this story now because I want all of you—and I do mean all—to know that I wasn't always a somewhat-overweight woman without an upper lip to her name who can occasionally be found sleeping behind her face and always thinking in her mouth. I was once a relevant piece of ass who barely knew she existed while much of the rest of the moviegoing world saw me romping through the air in a metal bikini, awake as I needed to be in order to slay space slugs, being whoever I needed to be in the face of affective disorders and otherwise.

I can now share this with others because the story is part of history. It's so long ago, it winds up being a real workout for my memory. This is an episode that's only potentially interesting because its players became famous for the roles they were playing when they met.

Harrison is a decent—albeit complicated and frequently silent—guy. He's always been decent to me, and as far as I know the only time he cheated on any one of his three wives was with me. And maybe he didn't think that counted all that much because of how short I am.

So while there's still time for Carrison to grow old together, that gateway is steadily closing. If we're going to get back together we're going to have to do it soon. And getting back together with someone you were never truly with is, to say the least, complicated. But absolutely worth the effort. Or not. I'll probably regret writing this, but if you have the impulse to yell at me, please don't. Periodically, I feel guilty enough on my own.

My hopes aren't high, and neither, as it happens, am I.

FIRE SALE
Welchade
FRUIT PUNCH

luminous beings were we

In the beginning, when *Star Wars* became a bona fide phenomenon, none of us knew how to be famous (maybe Harrison or Mark did, but if so, they weren't sharing their insights with me). They didn't offer that class at Berlitz, and we lacked a manual containing suggestions on how to edge into this transitional state smoothly. Yes, I know I should've been able to access what was expected of me by watching my mother and elusive part-time father, which I would've done had I anticipated a life like theirs—which was in fact lifelike—but remember, I knew I would never go into such a fickle business.

It all happened so quickly. Instantly there was a lot of fan mail, and we initially read all of it ourselves.

As I've said, I had known celebrity before in connection with the tabloid frenzy surrounding my parents, so I wasn't exactly swimming in unfamiliar waters. But having watched their fame diminish over the course of their lifetimes had taught me the limit of fame. You could clutch the tail of this wild tiger but you had to know—or at least I knew—that at some point it would wrest itself from your desperate grasp and hightail it off to someone else's jungle.

Besides, this *Star Wars* fame meant that Princess Leia was famous and not Carrie Fisher. I just happened to look like her—minus her bad hair, and plus less conspicuous bad hair all my own. I think fame might be more fun when it's personal and not just someone remarking how trippy it is that you look so much like that *Star Wars* character. It's still fun, though, don't get me wrong. Or do. I can't stop you.

I'd had what I always referred to as associative fame. By-product fame. Fame as the salad to some other, slightly more filling main dish. Celebrity-daughter fame (and later, when married to Paul Simon, celebrity-wife fame). And now, with *Star Wars*, I had that happened-to-have-played-an-iconic-character fame. Still, being newly famous in whatever way you were famous was a very busy business. The main task at hand was showing people that I was just as independent and likable as was the intergalactic princess I portrayed.

I think boys may have been attracted to my accessibility. Even if I did have some princessy qualities, I wasn't conventionally beautiful and sexy, and as such was less likely to put them down or think I was too good for them. I wouldn't humiliate them in any way. Even if I teased them in the context of running around with laser guns dodging bullets, I wouldn't do it in a way that would hurt them.

What is happening? How did we get here? Where *is* here? How long will it last? What *is* it? Do I deserve it? What does this make me? What do you wear to an event like that? What do you think I should say? What if I don't know the answer? Being around my mom when she was being recognized was hardly an effective preparation for any of this.

Fame can be incredibly intense, and of course none of us had any idea that anything like it would ever happen. You'd have to be a psychic of a very unique Hollywood sort to guess something of this order was up ahead ready to ambush you, transforming the character you played into a household name. The studio would set up a tour, a press junket, which was what you did especially for a movie like this where the cast were virtual unknowns. Then the movie came out and everybody went wild. Suddenly this little movie needed no promotion. But because no one could ever have anticipated that, we ended up doing the junket anyway, which became the definition of overkill. But whatever it was, it turned out that wherever we went, people were waiting and they all seemed very happy to have us there, selling the sold.

We'd done this little low-budget film. They'd even flown us economy to our location in London to save money, and we lived off a per diem that came nowhere near the vicinity of luxurious. We'd done a cool little off-the-radar movie directed by a bearded guy from Modesto. A thing like that wasn't going to make people want to play with a doll of you, was it?

It was *one movie*. It wasn't supposed to do what it did—nothing was supposed to do *that*. Nothing ever had. Movies were meant to stay on the screen, flat and large and colorful, gathering you up into their sweep of story, carrying you rollicking along to the end, then releasing you back into your unchanged life. But this movie misbehaved. It leaked out of the theater, poured off the screen, affected a lot of people so deeply that they required endless talismans and artifacts to stay connected to it.

Had I known it was going to make that loud of a noise, I would've dressed better for those talk shows and definitely would have argued against that insane hair (although the hair was, in its own modest way, a big part of that noise). And I certainly wouldn't have ever just blithely signed away any and all merchandising rights relating to my image and otherwise.

And on top of whatever else, Mark, Harrison, and I were the only people who were having this experience. So who do you talk to that might understand? Not that that is some sort of tragedy—it just puts you in an underpopulated, empathy-free zone. I mean, obviously I'd never starred in a movie, but this was completely not like starring in your average everyday movie. It might've been like being one of the Beatles. Sure, most of it was a fun surprise, but the days where you could really let your guard down were over because now there were cameras everywhere. I had to comport myself with something approaching dignity, at *twenty.*

But when we first began getting fan mail *forty years ago*, it was complicated to know what to do. Do you answer every letter or ignore some of the less enthusiastic? So for the first few months we all—that's *all*, Harrison, Mark, and I—answered every letter. How I know this is because we all received a letter from the mother of a little girl who was going blind and who had seen *Star Wars* with her last sight and would we send her daughter an autographed picture of ourselves before she went blind altogether. So the three of us promptly hurried off and sent her the letter before she lost her sight and somehow we all ended up discovering that little Lisa was a 20-20-sighted woman of sixty-three, causing us one of many laughs in our giddy days of early fame.

• • •

None of us had done talk shows before, so we were forced to develop not only our public personas but our talk show styles as we went from one to the next, touting the film that needed no tout. A tout-free experience, we should've informed the hosts before lining up like tin ducks at a carnival waiting to be shot. And shot we were—by televised film cameras all over the U.S. and eventually onward overseas.

I noticed right away that Harrison tended to quote philosophers when describing what he thought of the film. "As Winston Churchill said, 'Success is not final, failure is not fatal: it is the courage to continue that counts,'" he might've said when asked if he thought success would change us. He also might've said, "Give me a minute—I've only been successful for a few weeks." He might've said these things, but I'm pretty sure he didn't. But whatever he said shamed me. Why wasn't I quoting philosophers? Because I dropped out of high school midway through the eleventh grade. Well, when you really came right down to it (not similar to down to earth—or earthlings), being a dropout was a good reason to tune in and turn on—but it was no excuse for not quoting philosophers on daytime talk shows. (Mike Douglas *loves* philosophers!) People on *The Dating Game* misquoted the greatest minds of all time. "The unintentional life is not worth believing," Harrison might've said, and still gotten chosen as bachelor number three!

After a few shows of listening to Harrison waxing philosophical, I decided to take action. Harrison had majored in philosophy in college—what could I do to remain undaunted? Then it came to me: I would consult with a college professor in philosophy! And not just any college—I called Sarah Lawrence in suburban New York and asked if there was a professor whom I could consult with. They seemed hesitant until I mentioned *Star Wars* and implied I might soon share the screen with an intergalactic great mind known as Yoda, who would of course intone, "Do. Or do not. There is no try." As far as doing went, that seemed to do the trick.

Not that the higher-ups at Sarah Lawrence are any less susceptible to *Star Wars* any more than the average—or above-average—human. Which is to say that they were more flexible regarding the possibility of securing a professor for insecure me. Having had a few tutorials in philosophy, I believe I found one or two talk shows where I could employ my new college-level insights, but quickly determined that to have two actors spouting philosophical gems to the moviegoing public was a bit much—a bit of smuggler monkey see, princess monkey do.

So after a very short while, I gave up on looking intelligent, thank God, and I continue that to this day. I would make it look like a devious plan when I seemed less than effervescent and approaching pedestrian (without a crosswalk). You couldn't accuse me of doing a less-than-stellar job on the Johnny Carson show without my insisting that you had forgotten my telling you that that had been my intention all along.

We did so many chat shows that we finally wound up being overexposed. There are worse tragedies, but you couldn't have gotten me to guess what they were at the time. But we plodded along, newly minted celebrities gracing television shows all over America. We didn't realize initially how big a hit the movie was because we were traveling to every capital in every state promoting it—which you do when a film is an unknown quantity. It was being on the run and feeling as though I was trying to either keep up with something or keep away from some danger at my heels. But then bodies in motion tend to stay in motion—so that's where we stayed: in motion and on the road.

To relax in our giddy unrelaxed configurations, we would sometimes go to amusement parks. I remember one particular day in Seattle where Harrison—well, all of us really—had gotten on a Ferris wheel that had cages for seats that tended to spin as it went around. As you can see, it's difficult to describe—but the bottom upside-down line is that Mark and I had gotten on the ride first, so when we got off we watched as Harrison—who like all of us was still wearing what we'd worn on TV (not your optimum style for Disneyland Lite)—got on. And Mark and I stood on the ground laughing while a poker-faced Harrison hung upside down like a dressed-up fruit bat with a tie casually draped over his very serious face!

In some ways this whirling around made us look and feel like what our lives looked and felt like. I don't know, you had to be there. "There" being everywhere all at once—the traveling snake oil salesmen of space travel.

"Hurry, hurry, hurry. Step right up, everybody, and see this new, once-in-a-lifetime product I call the *Star Wars*—a tale of intergalactic excitement, with battle sequences and heroes and smugglers and princesses all careening through space having the time of their lives. And now you can have the time of your life—for the low, low price of five bucks, you too will have the time of your moviegoing, going, gone life! Hurry, hurry, hurry, act now because this deal will only be offered . . ." And on and on we went from state to state, capital to capital, audience to audience, hawking our wares and frequently not knowing where we were.

For me, the worst part of this better-than-best time period was when I was being photographed. I *hate* having my picture taken—maybe because it was already happening at the age of six hours, well before I was old enough to articulate my objections with words. I was forced to protest with infant expressions and baby poison eye darts. I hated it all through my childhood—when it shouldn't have been that big of a trial because I was young and cute (even *really* cute, depending on who you talk to)—and I *loathe* it now. Especially in this smartphone era, when anyone at any moment can take a candid shot somewhere when you're far from "camera ready" (i.e., most of the time), and you know it's not just a bad picture but a scornful reminder of just how old you're getting and how fat you've gotten—not only a reminder of what you once were but also of what you no longer are and never will be again. And, as if that wasn't enough, some stranger *owns* this horrific image and is free to do whatever with it in private or with his friends.

The movie had been out for a few weeks and the lines were twisting around the blocks. (The term "blockbuster," in fact, was born because ticket lines would come to the edge of the street, pause for that asphalt interruption, and then begin again enthusiastically on the next block.) I would drive by with my friends in disbelief, wondering how anything that popular could include me.

One day we were driving down Wilshire Boulevard in Westwood, where the Avco Cinema had what looked to me like the longest line I had seen so far. As you can imagine, I was really excited—"chuffed" is the British word for it. I love how they made themselves this little word that means "giddy with an excitement that you're trying to suppress because you'd rather be thought of as looking kind of cool." So I stood up on the car seat, and not just stuck out my head but squeezed half my body through the sunroof, then shouted, "Hey, I'm in that! I'm the princess!"

This certainly caused some interest, ranging from the scornful "What an asshole" variety to the breathless "Do you think it's really her?"

"I'm in that!" I repeated for those who hadn't heard me the first time. Then, suddenly realizing what I had done and quickly fearing that some of these moviegoers might identify me, I slid back down into my seat and said to my friend, "Quick! Drive!" So she stepped on the gas and sped away.

The one question people can never seem to stop asking me is "Did you know *Star Wars* was going to be that big of a hit?" Well, given that there had never actually been a film that had been that big of a hit before, who could possibly ever have assumed that there now would be?

Now I've begun answering that question differently than replying, "No I didn't." I've begun saying, "Well, actually, I thought it was going to be an even bigger phenomenon. So when it wasn't—when *Star Wars* and its sequels failed to meet my remarkable, almost unbelievable expectations—well, I want you to just try to imagine how crushed, how *disappointed* I felt, and still feel."

Imagine how it felt when my anticipated dreams and fantasies failed to come true. What would you have done if you were me? Turn to drugs, maybe? Lose your mind? Possibly maybe even both?

leia's lap dance

"Could you make it to Jerry? He couldn't come today. He's having chemo. But he's been your biggest fan since he was knee-high. We showed him the movies when he was three. JERRY. With a J, yes, that's right. And could you write, 'May the Force be with you'? You have no idea what this would *mean* to him. When I told him you were going to be here he *cried* . . . Thank you *so* much. He absolutely worships *Star Wars*.

"I just can't believe it's *you*. If someone told me back when I first saw the first episode, if someone had said, 'One day you're gonna meet Princess Leia face-to-face,' I just wouldn'ta . . . I woulda thought you was making fun of me, ya know? Back then . . . *agghh*, I am *so* sorry, a grown woman standing here cryin' like a baby, you must think I'm plumb loco... No, that's okay, I've gotten to where it doesn't bother me as much what people think of me. I mean, it still hurts but not so much so's I'm useless.

"And part of that's 'cause of you. Princess Leia was such a huge inspiration to me. I thought, if *I* could grow up and be even just a *little* like you! 'Cause a little of you looked like a big ole lot to me. And then when I grew up, or got older, whichever, and I was on the express checkout line reading the magazine while I was waitin' for the people with twenty items when you're not supposed to have more than a dozen, so while I'm waitin' I'm flippin' through this magazine and I come across this picture of you. I might not've known it was you, except there was a picture of you in the slave outfit on the opposite page.

"So I start reading, and I swear I came to think that my finding that magazine with you in it was no accident. I don't know if you put much... you know, I doubt you believe in God or whatnot, 'cause I've always heard that celebrities are... You do?... Oh, well, whatever you wanna call Him or It or...

"Look at me, here I am just rattlin' off at the mouth when you have so many other people waiting, I'll just shut my trap and let you get to them, but before I do, could I ask you one last little favor? A picture? I mean, how many times does somebody find themselves standing with... I'm sorry, I get to talking, I'm just so *thrilled* and so *nervous* to meet you. Wait'll I tell Ira down at the blood bank, he said I'd probably never...

"My camera? It's in my purse. I *think*, I *HOPE*! Wouldn't that be... as my mom used to say, wouldn't that *beat all*? I wish she were still alive. She passed right when the first *Star Wars* came out. I remember at her wake my cousins were talking about this crazy-sounding movie that had just opened that Wednesday. Amazing, isn't it?

"At first it was just *super* hard for me, and if it hadn't been for *Star Wars*, I swear I don't know if I would've made it. It was like, God took my mom home to Him and He led me to *Star Wars*. He gave me you and Luke and Han, and somehow that was enough. I don't mean 'enough' like having *Star Wars* was like having my mom back to life and stitchin' one of her crazy embroideries or . . . or . . . That makes her sound like some kinda Betty Crocker–type mom and that's something she just absolutely sure as shit, 'scuse my French, wasn't. She was a lotta things, my mom—my brother could tell you. He'd a been here but he couldn't get off work. Me and him, we used to follow my mom without her knowin' to make sure she was, well, that she'd keep outta trouble 'n' such... I'm sorry, what?... Oh, Ben. That's my brother's name, Ben. Like Ben Kenobi, only not, 'cause like I said she died before she coulda seen it. That's one regret I have. I don't like focusing on regretting things much, but I truly believe that if my mom coulda seen you guys's movies she… Well, no use cryin' over spilt people.

"How's your mom these days? I was sorry to hear about your dad. Did you and he ever… Picture? Oh yes, *please*. Is there someone who could take it so we're both in it? Otherwise people won't believe me when I . . . Oh, would you? Aren't you sweet! You just press here after you get it all framed right… Okay, now, one sec… Is there any way you could put your arm around me? You can say no, I just had to . . . Aren't you sweet? I will never *ever* forget this day, even without the picture… Okay, are we framed in the center? You sure? Okay, hold real still… *Cheese!*"

The word "autograph" comes to us originally from the Greek *autos*, "self," and *graphos*, "written": self-written. As it is popularly used, it refers to a famous person's signature. The hobby of collecting autographs—the practice of hoarding such mementos, which are often wrenched enthusiastically (if not savagely) from the hands of "celebrities"—is known as philography (or occasionally, "unpleasant").

Some of the more sought-after signers are, in no particular order, presidents, military heroes, sports icons, actors, singers, artists, religious and social leaders, scientists, astronauts, authors, and Kardashians.

So. A keepsake, coaxed or inveigled from a celebrity by someone eagerly radiant, glowing with the recognition of a familiar face. A face as familiar as the closest of friends or family, and yet this familiarity is completely one-sided.

I grew up watching my mother signing autographs, writing her name on smiling photos of herself, or on pieces of blank paper hopefully held out to her by the outstretched arms of strangers who loved her. Her fans. The *Oxford English Dictionary* says the word "fan" derives, quite apparently, from the word "fanatic," which means "marked by excessive enthusiasm and often intense uncritical devotion."

The entirety of what Debbie Reynolds knew of her fans is that they seriously appreciated her talents. They invested tiny pieces of their souls in her. When my father dumped her for Elizabeth Taylor, leaving her squirming sadly in the world's spotlight with two bewildered toddlers, they shared her pain.

That sort of familiarity bred quite the opposite of contempt, though something equally charged. In a way she belonged to the world, and while most of the portion of it that appreciated her was content to do so at a distance, the true fans seemed to want to assert a kind of ownership by coyly requesting, or pitifully pleading, or aggressively demanding, that she provide them with their coveted token, proof to all and for all time, in the pre-selfie era, of an encounter! An up-close brush with one of the cinematically anointed!

I would stand loyally at my mother's side, watching as these memento-seeking well-wishers (MSW2s) gushed and giggled in her presence. From just outside her dazzle of limelight, I watched as she scribbled her lovely signature on the pictures, records, and magazines—many of their covers blaring "news" of the scandal she'd been subjected to—that were sometimes desperately held out to her.

"And what's your name? Oh, what a lovely name! So unusual! Do you spell it with a 'y' or an 'ie'?" "I had an Aunt Betty once. I loved her very much." "Yes, but only if you take the picture very quickly. As you can see, I'm with my daughter…"

"Your daughter?!!" these devotees would exclaim, briefly wrenching their eyes toward me. "That's right! You have a daughter! Oh, my goodness, I didn't realize she'd gotten so *big*, and a beauty like her mama!"

I'd frown and look away. This wasn't supposed to happen. I was there as an observer, not the observed. A witness to the world's mysteries. The archaeologist, not the pit. I'd blush and tuck my chin toward my chest as the focus abruptly shifted to me, caught off guard, in the act.

"Isn't she precious?"

• • •

I can't remember exactly when I started referring to signing autographs for money as a celebrity lap dance, but I'm sure it didn't take me long to come up with it. It's lap dancing without cash being placed in any underwear, and there's no pole—or is the pole represented by the pen?

It is certainly a higher form of prostitution: the exchange of a signature for money, as opposed to a dance or a grind. Instead of stripping off clothes, the celebrity removes the distance created by film or stage. Both traffic in intimacy.

For many years I, like so many other high-minded celebrities with flourishing careers, could afford to cavalierly wave away any and all arguably undignified appearance offers that, accompanied by a financial enticement, could only be experienced by those engaging in said ignoble acts as, for want of a better word, whoring.

To be sure, it is "selling out," which comes with feelings of embarrassment and shame. But if you're selling for high enough numbers, the duration of that humiliation has a more fleeting quality. And the distraction of purchasing the odd luxury item, or—saints preserve us—paying bills, made the sense of shame similar to the embarrassment one feels about a weight gain of a fairly manageable variety.

And then, what is a loss of self-respect when placed in the context of diminishing worry about one's looming tax bill or monstrous overhead? So, over time I have managed to rejigger my definition of dignity to the point where it comfortably includes lap dancing.

It's just something that had to be gotten used to—like finding out your older sister is actually your mother, or winning the lottery but only being able to spend the money on Christmas Day. Hardly a hardship—it simply took some form of adaptation. With enough time, anything can be adjusted to, though things like torture would require adjustment of a kind I can scarcely imagine. But accustoming myself to scrawling my name for strangers was certainly within my capacities.

Besides, over time, more and more celebrities have lent their overly familiar names and faces to products of all kinds—from cars to cosmetics to soda, and on into that netherworld just beyond yogurt. Nothing in the ever-evolving world of celebrity endorsement was impossible. So, why should I be ashamed of spending days on end signing eight-by-ten photos of myself, or even signing the flesh of another human who would subsequently get that signature tattooed onto their skin for all time? Why should that embarrass me more than Julia Roberts or Brad Pitt endorsing some high-end perfume that everyone knows they're not wearing, or Penélope Cruz appearing in a commercial swooning over cappuccino?

Well, there are reasons, the biggest one being that getting seventy dollars per signature doesn't really compare to the millions the likes of Mr. Pitt or Ms. Roberts receive for a photo shoot lasting a few hours. The difference might be compared to turning tricks in the East Village versus giving a hand job to an appreciative duke or duchess.

When I was initially approached about going to Comic-Con, the giant comic book convention, I said, "I wouldn't be caught *dead* at one of those has-been roundups." But, as it turns out, I've been caught *alive* at those roundups often enough to wish I was dead.

"I don't like to make a practice of it, but just this once, okay, I'll sign it Princess Leia. But you do know I'm not *actually* her, right? I might resemble this character that doesn't really exist offscreen and in human form—well, maybe I don't resemble her quite as much as I *used* to, but for a while there I looked almost *exactly* like her."

"Could you make it to Zillondah? That's two Ls, an O before the N, and A-H at the end. One of the Ls is silent."

"Come on, get the fuck over yourself," I can hear you saying. "You wanted to be in show business. Deal with it!"

But I didn't! It's just that it turned out to be a lot harder to stay out of the famous fray than to enter it.

Perpetual celebrity—the kind where any mention of you

will interest a significant percentage of the public until the day you die, even if that day comes decades after your last real contribution to the culture—is exceedingly rare, reserved for the likes of Muhammad Ali.

Most celebrities have the ordinary variety, in which lengthening periods of quiet alternate with brief flare-ups of activity that steadily diminish in intensity and frequency until the starlight fades away entirely, ultimately extinguished, at which point there's that final blaze of nostalgia that marks the passing of the now-lost icon.

So I knew. I knew that what lies ahead for almost every public figure who arrives on the scene lay ahead for me as well: the attempted comeback, the memoir, the stint(s) in rehab (although the option of lingering on in some reality show lineup didn't exist yet in the late seventies). I knew that this was just the nature of this unnatural business—that there, but for the bad fortune of someone else in stardom, would go me. I just hadn't come up with a viable alternative, so when my place in the sun presented itself, I didn't have the nerve to turn it down. And this wasn't just a gift horse, it was a gift stampede!

But, as inevitable as it is, you know some people think it will last forever. That beautiful actress over there, a bright young star from a newly successful franchise, beaming happily, or wait, maybe not so happily.

"I'm sorry, I don't have time to personalize," she tells the thrilled fan holding out a picture of her in a bikini, lying on a beach under a tropical sun.

The fan's brow furrows. "But I've been waiting for almost two hours," he pleads. "Couldn't you just—"

"NO!" she snaps, indicating the long line snaking behind him. "They've been waiting just as long as you!" She's fed up at all these eager devotees *crowding* her. "One of them stepped on my foot! See?!!" The beautiful actress frowns, indicating a little red mark on her ankle. "Oww," she adds for emphasis. "How much longer do I have to stay?" she asks her handler, her eyes stormy.

The handler leans down to her nervously, his head covered in sweat. "We've cut the line at the east entrance. All you have to do is sign for those who got in before the cut. It shouldn't take you *that* long. Can I get you a water? Or a snack or something?"

The beautiful actress rolls her eyes impatiently. "Christ," she mumbles under her fragrant breath, "get me some fries then. Or an apple crepe."

Her handler breathes a sigh of relief. "You got it! No worries, I'll be back in a second." The beautiful actress smirks, shakes her head moodily, and turns back to the nervously waiting fan. She blinks at him.

"Didn't I sign your thing already?" she barks, frightening him speechless. "Well, didn't I?"

Wry and resigned, her older counterparts watch from

behind their photo-laden tables in this cavernous convention center, armed only with their pens and their stoic grins, on the dark sides of their once bright, shining stars, their focus-pulling days all but over, not to mention their days in general—*there's Bill Shatner*!

Spending much less time signing than waiting to oblige the next long-lost fan in search of a nostalgic signature. Signing photos taken when they were still certain it all lay ahead, their brilliant multicolored futures, populated with throngs of admirers who clung to their every motion, hung on their every word. The staring world barely blinked then. Now it dozes.

Such is the fate that awaits all celebrities, poor dears. Waiting for an audience either no longer living or barely interested, making every effort to seem upbeat as they await the day when their fans will return to them, their current indifference having been merely a result of some temporary misunderstanding soon to be resolved.

Until then, all they have to do is pretend it's not really happening.

"No, I'm sorry, I can't do it that weekend. I've got a lap dance in San Diego."

It was such an obvious metaphor to me—metaphor be with you!—that it was easy to forget that it wasn't an accepted designation in the common vernacular. Sure, my friends and family got the reference, but all too often I'd forget that I wasn't sufficiently acquainted with someone who'd only very recently wandered into the eccentric entrance hall of my life. Such as, for example, some place of business where, confronted with the price tag of an overpriced item, I'd say, "Shit, I can't afford that until after my lap dance next month."

I'd continue along breezily for a sentence or two until I'd notice the look of astonishment on the high-end shop assistant's face. "Sorry, sorry," I'd explain. "I don't mean an actual lap dance, though it might as well be. It's this thing where I sign stuff for cash that is all but stuffed into my underwear and—oh, never mind, it doesn't—could you hold this for me for a few weeks?"

It's fair to conclude that my lap dancing was required penance for my fondness for shopping—either for gifts for my friends and mere acquaintances, or for yet another amusing antique hand or eye or foot, some gnome, some video art, some British phone booth for my witty and colorful home. (I have the mixed blessing of being able to find the often obscurely hidden charm in many arguable objets d'art, not to mention animals and humans.)

If I didn't simply *have* to have things—and to make a donation to this cause, or a loan (inadvertently but inevitably a gift) to that person—I might not have needed to clamor to this city or that country to do the odd speech or the odder-still autograph show.

I was decidedly on the wrong side of forty when, as the new millennium dawned, I was first approached by Ben Stevens (with Official Pix) to see if I would consider doing "a signing." My nose wrinkled involuntarily with distaste. Don't you have to be *desperate* to do something like sitting behind some table piled high with pics and pens and . . . would there be *merch*, even?!!

Ben smiled compassionately. "There's *no* merchandising," he said emphatically, as if to assure me that this lack of obvious commerce would keep my dignity intact. "Just signing pictures, and if you wanted to make a little extra moolah, you could take a few photos with the fans. No more than fifty, unless you wanted to do more. Mainly, though, me and my staff would be there to make sure things go smoothly and quickly and, of course, that you make as much money as possible."

How did I get here? I didn't need money *this* badly, did I? Well, that all depends on your definition of "need." Was I as rich as most of the media-saturated public assumed that I was, given that I was associated with one of the biggest moneymaking phenomena in the life of the nation? Not by a long, long, long shot. Holding out for points or a piece of the merchandising was not an option for—or even something that would ever have occurred to—a nineteen-year-old signing on for her first lead role in a little space movie.

To be sure, though, I had a considerable amount of money in my early twenties. Wow! Then I didn't have to think about such things. I could pay someone to make sure my bills were paid and my money was locked up tight and under no immediate threat of theft. Great! My attitude was, "You take care of it! Just make sure that I can shop and travel as much as possible. I'm no good with numbers, so you count while I cavort!" Carefree!

That went well.

Two decades and a pilfering business manager later, I was out of money. My house—or, more accurately, the house the bank lets me live in, for now—was mortgaged to the skies, and not, as it turned out, friendly ones.

I had become a poor rich person. Cavorting in the style I had unfortunately become accustomed to now required real work. I took jobs writing travel pieces for magazines so I could circle the globe, my young daughter in tow.

When Billie was four or five, I made personal appearances at every Disneyland on the planet. (All she knew was that we didn't have to stand in lines and got to go on the Matterhorn three times and have lunch with Dumbo!) So, while I might not yet have lost my convention virginity when Ben Stevens came a-calling, I was far from an innocent in the ways of selling myself, or at least my-Leia-self.

Your once upon a time is up
Prince Charming's been abducted
Tinkerbell's on angel dust
The Matterhorn's erupted

Your once upon a time is up
Tammy's talking dirty,
Dumbo has a PhD
Leia's age is 2 x 30

There we are in the huge, almost football-field-sized convention center. Many of us, side by side at long tables in front of longer swaths of blue fabric—curtains of blue separating the celebrities from . . . what? From round tables piled high with different sorts and sizes of photographs.

We have gone on—aged, and in some cases (like my own) waists have thickened a bit—but the images have not changed. In the photos we are stopped in our tracks, usually in a scene from a past film, caught for all time smiling or swooning, gazing or considering. And just beneath that momentary expression—that split second out of all the years of our lives—a signature will, for a nominal or near-nominal fee, be scrawled. That souvenir, now yours forever, captures two instants: the long-ago one when the photo was taken, and the more recent one when that signature was written just for you—you or some lucky friend or relative whose life you've generously chosen to enhance in this way. Two moments, decades apart, now joined forever.

We sit in various stages of poised, awaiting our next appointment to exchange autograph for cash—yes, actual paper money, the kind that they're promising to put a picture of a woman on one of these years. That cash entitles people to choose what color ink should be used—the table is festooned with a rainbow of available pens—and which character's name they might also want inscribed below the actor's signature. Oh, and perhaps also a key line of dialogue spoken by said character?

Finally, and for many most importantly, the ability to carve out a uniquely personal exchange between the lap dancer and lap dancee, something so easily documented in the smartphone era. At the very least a selfie, but even better a video of your idol engaging you—*you!*—in actual conversation. A digital keepsake that you will be able to carry with you and show off—to those, one hopes, who will share your enthusiasm rather than react with an air of endurance—until the end of time, or at least until such time as you lose the phone that you foolishly neglected to back up the contents of and realize that you have lost not only your phone but also proof of your contact with stardom.

But there will be another Comic-Con—they're hardly rare now—where, if your luck with luminaries prevails, you will again find yourself in (or, more accurately, maneuver yourself into) immediate proximity to your chosen celebrity's latest lap dance, which is when you can say, "Hey, Carrie, it's me, Jeffrey Altuna! We met at last year's Florida Con! I was with that girl Corby with the Slave Leia tattoo on her shoulder! Yeah! Right! How you been? We're down here visiting friends in Houston and, lucky me, this is the weekend for *this*. And anyway, Cheryl, that's my wife—say hey, honey—anyway . . . hell, I lost my train of whatever I was saying . . . Only that it's great to see you again. And Gary! Hey, boy! Tongue still hanging down, I see. Gosh almighty, he is *so* cute! We have a Westie-poodle mix—my oldest calls it a Woodle—and we love him to bits, but he's just nowhere near as bright as your little man here. You get him a Twitter page like you said you wanted to? Instagram! Better still! How awesome! Does he have many followers?? 41k?! That's more than most humans! I'll follow him right away! What's his name on it? Gary Fisher @garyfisher! That's brilliant! How did you think of it? . . . I'm kidding! What do you think I am?? Some fan moron? No, I'm totally kidding again! We are just big fans. We love you for just being who you are—maybe not regular, but not *not regular*, you know? I hope I'm not talking too much—guess I am 'cause of how Cheryl's looking at me, she's got my number, but could I ask you something? And I'm not talking about some super-dark secret inside scoop or anything because

I know you're not allowed to say, but my neighbor Bob reads up on all this and he reckoned that the black boy's skin is dark because of some hex that the Dark Side puts on him. Is that true? If yes, just nod your . . . I know, I know. I'm sorry—I just promised Bob I'd ask you if I saw you, and well, here we are! I couldn't let an opportunity like this just—*boom!*—swish by, right? I mean sure, no, yeah, I see that's quite a line, I'll let you go. I just wanted, I'm just glad to see you again like this and I gotta say, we are *really* looking forward to the opening on December eighteenth. Can't wait! Okay, bye, Gary! Take good care of your mama now—ya hear? Bye now!"

I need you to know that I'm not cynical about the fans. (If you thought I was, you would quite properly not like me, which would defeat the purpose of this book and of so much else that I do.) I'm moved by them.

There's something incredibly sweet and mystifying about people waiting in lines for so long. And with very few exceptions, the people you meet while lap dancing are a fine and darling lot. The *Star Wars* films touched them in some incredibly profound or significant way. They remember *everything* about the day they first saw *Star Wars* one, two, and three (which were officially, of course, *IV*, *V*, and *VI*): where they were, who they were with, what obstacles they had to overcome—cut school? skip practice?—in order to be there. And once they got there, how the experience surpassed any expectations they might have had, resulting in some life-changing experience. How, that day, things for them ceased to be in any way the same from then to forever after.

So of course when they meet me, many of the Forever Altered long to tell me all these things and more, and at length.

There's the girl with my signature tattooed to her ass, the couple that named their child Leia Carrie, the guy who had his name legally changed to Luke Skywalker. (Imagine the policeman's face when he stops Luke Skywalker for speeding: "What happened, Obi-Wan wouldn't let you use the X-wing fighter tonight?") They have marriage ceremonies where, instead of the more traditional vows, one says, "I love you," and the other says, "I know." They come dressed in the outfits, and not only are the women in the metal bikini but some men are wearing it, too, and it looks fantastic.

For the most part they're kind and courteous, and as if that weren't enough, they quite frequently appear before you in amazing homemade costumes whipped up by Alderaan-obsessed parents for their Force-fed children. Tiny Ben Kenobis, little Lukes, miniature Darth Vaders, and—my personal favorites—the teensiest of Princess Leias.

These smallest of small Leias are brought to me like tiny offerings, prize possessions held aloft for my blessings and my praise, both of which they receive in abundance. Do the children know that it's "me" that they are dressed as? Of course not! Those under four—all *they* know is that they're hot, that there are way too many people swarming around everywhere, and that they just want to go home, or anywhere other than standing in this line with similarly swaddled sorts spilling out of their sci-fi garb with no imminent sign of escape.

One little girl came by who'd been told she was going to meet Princess Leia; imagine her excitement, that is, until she saw the new me.

"No!" she wailed, squirming her head away from the sight of me. "I want the other Leia, not the old one."

Her father flushed, then leaned apologetically toward my ear. "Well, no, you see she doesn't mean that—we've just seen the first three films and loved you in them so much—"

"Please!" I interrupted. "You don't have to apologize for my looking older to your daughter after forty years. I look older to me, too, and I don't apologize to myself—though perhaps I should."

Vast airwaves of awkwardness ensued, his daughter unable to look at me and confront what time had done. It all ended well though, with me promising to get plastic surgery (after I explained to the little girl what that was) and getting her father to promise to read his daughter bits of *Wishful Drinking*, and look at its pictures together, so she'd see what the actual Carrie was like and how pretty she could be once the endlessly extraordinary Leia was finished.

The youngest fans who do know where they are (and where they're likely to be for quite some time) rarely seem happy, and when they finally reach their inexplicable destination they become paralyzed with shyness and hide behind whatever part of their parents they can access through their stormtrooper getups. The most desperate, confused, or hungry ones cry in fear or embarrassment or exasperation, or all three, while I do my best to soothe them. I bust my ass trying to soothe them, for their pain is palpable and I have rampant empathy.

And while the adults are unfailingly polite, there's a certain lack of empathy among some of them for me. They know they might be bothering me with their requests—a selfie, a lengthy inscription, an extra few "for my friends, they love *Star Wars* as much as I do, one of them even more"—and they're quick to acknowledge this and pretend that they could accept rejection. But fuck it, they know they're not asking me to do anything that hard. They present their requests with the pretense that I have the option to refuse, but we're all aware that the exchange could move very quickly to, "Well, you wanted to be in show business, and if you didn't want people to want your autograph you should never have become an actress."

They also frequently want you to write a piece of dialogue, and that is how I first came to understand who they thought Leia was. I knew who she was to the women, but the men really liked her unthreatening little bitchiness, which was probably even less intimidating because I'm short. All the lines they want me to write are like "Aren't you a little short for a stormtrooper?" The biggest favorite is "Why, you stuck-up, half-witted, scruffy-looking nerf herder." They can't get enough of it.

I sit there in front of all of these different pictures of myself from a million years ago and attempt to make looking at images from other eras somehow interesting to me. I don't remember when these photos were taken or who the photographers were. One picture in particular makes me feel happy and sad—it's a very popular one, and in it I look high as a kite. I occasionally like to ask people, "How do I look in that shot?" The kinder people respond "sleepy" or "tired" or "almost available."

I was signing my nude-ass picture a decade or so ago and I realized that I'd been—and I can't believe I'm using this word about myself—a sex symbol. Only now the reaction I sometimes get is disappointment, occasionally bordering on resentment, for my having desecrated my body by letting my age increase so. It's like I've TPed myself, thrown eggs at myself, defaced myself as if I were a rowdy trick-or-treater, and some of them are appalled. I wish I'd understood the kind of contract I signed by wearing something like that, insinuating I would and will always remain somewhere in the erotic ballpark appearance-wise, enabling fans to remain connected to their younger, yearning selves—longing to be with me without having to realize that we're both long past all of this in any urgent sense, and accepting it as a memory rather than an ongoing reality.

It is truly an honor to have been the first crush of so many boys. It's just difficult to get my head around having spent so much time in so many heads—and that time was of a certain quality. It occurred to me one day, as I finished affixing my flowery signature to yet another photograph of my long-ago young self wearing that slave bikini, that it could appear as though someone had convinced me that if I signed enough of these provocative images, I would at some point magically return to being young and slim.

"You were my first crush." I heard it so much I started asking who their second one was. We know what a first crush is to a teenager, but what does it mean to a five-year-old?

"But I thought you were mine! That I had found you—I was the only one who knew how beautiful you were—because you weren't beautiful in that usual way women in film are, right?"

He realizes that I might take what he's saying wrong. He doesn't mean it that way. I reassure him, touch his arm;

why not give him an anecdote? "I know what you mean, it's fine. Go on."

He checks my face to see if I mean it. I do. He continues, "So my friend, when I tell him about my crush, he goes, 'Oh yeah, she's awesome! I have a total crush on her, too. Everyone does.' I got upset. I coulda punched him."

"Why?"

"Because you were mine and I wanted to be the one who loved you. Me, maybe even help you . . ." He got embarrassed. "Anyway—I wanted to tell you." He shrugs, then adds, "Thanks for my childhood," and walks off. Wow, what a thing to be given credit for, to be thanked for! Because he didn't mean his whole childhood—he meant the good bits. The parts he escaped to. I'm grateful for those good bits he shared with me. And this honor is one that should be and is shared massively and gratefully with George Lucas. And Pat McDermott.

We showed it to our daughter when she was five and we've been trying to figure out when to show it to our son, who's four and a half. What do you think?"

It's like they're introducing the child to a tribe; there's a ritual—you hold your child above your head, bring him toward some *Wizard of Oz*–like setup, place him down as an offering, and say, "Watch this." Then you watch him watching *Star Wars*, trying to find out how much you have in common with your kid, see which character he'll identify with, who he'll root for, and hope that at the end of it you can still love your child in the same way. (I showed it to Billie when she was five, and her first reaction was that it was too loud. Also her second and third.)

If you can find a common language that runs from five to eighty-five, you've got yourself something, and *Star Wars* fans have something. In a way, it's as if they know they have this great gift to bestow, and they want to bestow it as perfectly as possible—the perfect time, the perfect place, the perfect situation for passing on this life-defining experience. And the kids will always remember for their entire lives how they first felt when they first saw their now favorite movie. And they were given this gift from their parents, and can now share it together. Truly a family affair.

"My mother showed it to me when I was six," one mother says, "and it kick-started my life."

The women forgive me for being in the metal bikini because they know I'm not in it voluntarily, and they let the men like it—even have their fairly innocuous little erections—because they know that I represent something else and not just that sex thing. Capable, reliable, equal to if not better than a man. I'm sure I didn't pay enough attention to what things were like BL (Before Leia), but the movie came out at the same time as a popular slogan of the day,

"A woman without a man is like a fish without a bicycle," and many females of all ages seem to have been glad I'd arrived on the scene, a heroine for our time.

I was something women and men could agree on. They didn't like me in the same way, but they liked me with the same intensity, and were all fine with the other sex liking me, too. Isn't that weird? Think about it. And then stop and ponder something actually important.

Sorry, but could you use a silver pen? Great, thanks. And wait, not there, maybe in that space next to your head? That would be great. And could you write the character's name just under yours? PLO? What does that mean, Palestine something? Of course! Princess Leia Organa. Very funny. But could you maybe also just write Leia, like in parentheses or something? Thanks.

"This is so great, now I have pretty much everyone—once I get Harrison, I mean. Yeah, right, it sure is a long shot, but no harm in hoping, is there? I didn't think I'd get Mark in the beginning 'cause at first he wasn't doing them, and then all of a sudden they said he was going to that celebration in San Diego. At first I didn't believe—I thought I'd fall over. Not *fall* fall, but I was light-headed, woozy-like.

"I guess you've probably noticed by now that I am really kind of a fanatic. Yet even as I say it, I really don't feel, like, crazy. *Star Wars* gives me a feeling of... *ongoingness*, you know? Like it's been here, and it's still here, and it'll stay here. Especially now with the new movie coming out. I mean, when they first said there was going to be a new movie I just—wow. You know? Dreams really can come true. That's why I believe I'm going to get Harrison's autograph. Sure, the odds are kind of against it, but who thought there'd really be *Episode VII* and that you guys were going to be in it? That would've seemed crazy to a lot of people. Not me, though, 'cause I believe in it. Not like religion believe, that would be schizo, sort of, but also not *not* like religion. It's got good and evil like a religion and miracles and priests and devils.

"The thing about *Star Wars* for me is the characters. They feel so real to me, like you could know them if you met them. Like I'm talking to you. I always knew I'd talk to you one day. I don't know *how* I knew, I just did. When I first saw you in *A New Hope*—and when did they start calling it that anyway, when did it stop being just *Star Wars*?—it was like I'd seen you before. No, not in *Shampoo*, I was too young for that, but you were so familiar. Not in a creepy way familiar, but familiar like... like *family* familiar. Hey! Those words are practically the same, right?

"See, it's stuff like that! Stuff you didn't know you knew till... till it was like you'd never not known it. That's how I felt about *Star Wars*. About all of you guys in *Star Wars*.

You were my family. Sure, your branch of the tree was more special than my actual family, but because of you being amazing, maybe I could be amazing one day. And even if I wasn't, I was still related to awesome. To you.

"I saw myself in you, and that's why I can stand here and talk to you. Why I got over being nervous so fast. Because—well, I just said why. Because of the Force. Because it moves through you and around you and into the person standing across from you. It's like this thing my mom used to say: 'I salute the light of the God within you.' *That's* the Force for me. I salute the light of the Force within and without you. The light that shines away from the dark side. Whatever it is that the Force wills, I will. I will its will. Its will, not mine, be done. Give me the knowledge of the all-knowing Force—give me the power to carry out the will of the Force. I thank the Force for empowering me with the light that shines its forceful rays on me, through me, and to infinity. May this force be with us all.

"Sorry, I know I must sound wacky—to some people I sound wacky, to others I don't—but I can see that light in you, the light of the Force that unites us and binds us to see that we get to the next place. The one that waits for us, and that waiting is what many of us call safety. I feel the Force take my will and move it slowly and evermore its way, move me ever so radiantly into the next thing or things.

"And one of those things is *Episode VII*. I am a part of it just as it is of me. I've waited for it for *a very long time.* Those prequels weren't *Star Wars*—Jar Jar Binks, God! But *VII* is the epitome of *Star Wars.* I do its bidding and trust its direction. I pulse with each beat of the Force. Its strength is mine.

"I'm sorry, I didn't mean to go on like that. It happens when I get excited and . . . I don't? Well, I am. I mean, initially I was but then I must've gotten comfortable—for whatever reason I feel comfortable around you. The weird thing is that a bunch of my friends say I look like you. No, I know, you're not blond, but we have the same eye color—yeah, hazel. No? I thought they were . . . that's funny. Maybe I'm getting you mixed up with your mom—I read hers were green, but they look hazel in a bunch of her pictures. Did you know that only men can be color-blind? I didn't either!

"See, it's stuff like that. Almost everyone I know knew that, but I didn't, and now you didn't, too! You get a bunch of little things like that and it adds up, which might be why I remind my friends of you. When you were fat, I was fat, too! And then we had to lose weight—huh? No, Disney didn't send me a trainer. I guess they were just worried about you, they didn't need everyone who looked like you to lose weight, too. Did you also get that pre-diabetes thing? No? Maybe you still will—not that I hope that, I was just seeing how else we could be similar.

"The biggest thing for me was that it was because of you

I tried to become a lawyer. No, in the end I didn't, but at the time I thought, 'Hey, if Princess Leia can do everything she does, why can't I go to law school?' I had to do something that was the equivalent of when you yelled at Luke and Han, '*Put that thing away or you're gonna get us all killed!!!*'

"Ooooh, sorry. I didn't think it was gonna be that loud—I was just trying to do it like you. Yeah, I did, didn't I? I mean, was. I was as loud as you. Did it feel good when you did it? Okay, then! There's another thing! We both dieted, neither one of us is color-blind, and we feel good yelling. See, enough things eventually add up and—right, *no* girls are color-blind, but that doesn't matter 'cause so are we.

"Just like both of us having dogs named Gary! I didn't? I thought I told you that right away! Oh, well, then this is me telling you now. I have a dog named Gary, too! When? I don't know exactly but around the same time as you got your Gary. Maybe a little after, but I hadn't known about your Gary when I got mine. Or at least not *consciously*. You didn't Twitter it, did you? I thought not. All's I know is I had this crazy impulse one day to get a dog, right? I'd been super sick with really bad bronchitis—I had this really high fever, which made me get those super-vivid dreams, and in one dream I was with you and we both had this French bulldog named Gary. The weird thing was I didn't think I'd ever heard of that type of dog. Anyway, I dreamt we had this black bulldog and the next thing I know, my dad gets me this dog. Trippy, right? A lot of people thought I'd copied you, like always. But how could I have copied you when it was my dad that bought him for me based on a dream I can barely even still remember having?

"So that's just one more thing. You have to admit, there's something kind of spooky, no? We look alike, we have the same dog, almost the same hair color and weight issues. It adds up after a while, you have to admit. Some people might say it's coincidence, but even if it is it's a trippy coincidence.

"Hey! Maybe we can mate our Garys!!! No, my Gary is a girl, so it could work. Wouldn't that be awesome? I mean, that would be the perfect outcome to this whole snarl of amazingness! He is? Well, those things can be reversed, can't they? No? A dog can't be unfixed? But if you really believe he can, then he can! We could use the Force to unfix him, then have puppies we sell on Twitter! Or not sell. But announce the miracle. The Second Coming of... the Mating of Gary. Gary He and Gary She. Gary WE! We as in *oui*, which in French (as in French bulldog) means yes! So, yes! Bring on the bulldog babies!"

I saw where someone was complaining about how much celebrities charge for autographs at these events, and in our defense someone said, "Well, you know, it may cost that much now, but when she dies it's really going to be worth a lot." So my death is worth something to some people. If I had enough pictures signed someone could put out a hit on me.

Of course I also still sign autographs for free. At screenings, for example, where the professional autograph hounds follow you around, braying and nipping at your heels, waving photos under your face until someone whose signature is more valuable (or more current) shows up, at which point they abandon you until that brighter star escapes into a car or through a door, and then they come scampering back to you.

"Miss Fisher, please, I've flown all the way from Newfoundland!"

"Miss Fisher, please! I've been in love with you since I was a little boy!" (This man is in his sixties.)

"Miss Fisher, I was almost in 9/11." Well, then, you think, of course. This person could've been killed. Where do I sign? But then . . . wait. You think a second. What does that really mean? She was in the World Trade Center but somehow managed to escape? She was on the downtown subway stuck in midtown when the first plane hit? She'd interviewed for a job with Cantor Fitzgerald but didn't get it? She had a job there but slept through the sound of her alarm and so wasn't there at her desk when . . . And on and on and on.

But can you ask her any of this? More to the point, do you *want* to? Do you want to be the person questioning the validity of someone's tale of their brush with tragedy, just because you'd rather not sign their poster? But if it is a lie—if this woman has concocted this story to ensure that you'll not only sign her poster but that you'll sign four—hell, why not five? And for that matter, how about a grand total of eleven?

So if it's not true, and she's invented a story about narrowly escaping being somewhere horrific when she was really just home like the rest of us saps glued to the TV, then she just won the award for the fan most willing to lie about her involvement in one of the more sacred tragedies ever to scar this earth, and to risk hell for the sake of some sci-fi signature.

No. It couldn't be. Best not to think of it.

sensation adjacent

I went to Madame Tussauds to see the wax statue they'd made of me. Well, not me, actually. That would have been someone lying in bed watching old movies on TV, drinking a Coke with one hand while adjusting her dog Gary's tongue with the other. The statue they made was of Princess Leia me.

Not that I'm a big fan of my face, but still—it is mine, whichever way you tilt it. I didn't like my face when I should have and now that it's melted, I look back on that face fondly. People send me pictures of my young pre-melted face all the time. Angry pre-melted—a lot of angry pre-melted, actually. Agitated. Frustrated. My face tense with . . . well, mostly frustration.

But some of my expressions are happy. Super, beyond

happy. Stoned in some, most likely, but smiling, grinning my chin off. Gazing at some guy adoringly, both on-screen and off, sometimes simultaneously.

What expression did Madame Tussauds choose to embalm on my face? Impassive Leia/me. Staring stoically into the future with Jabba the Hutt giggling peacefully behind me. Why shouldn't he giggle? What's he got to worry about? Surely not his weight. He's big boned or no boned. He could do with some toning, but why bother? With impassive, sweaty-looking me as his slave and that annoying little rat in drag to amuse him, he's got a great life. One that Leia and I hope/plan to put an end to very shortly. But hey, we can plan all we want because now we're forever trapped in invisible amber, holding quite still so you can be photographed with all of us if you happen to be in the mood.

The main thing you notice, though, about wax Leia is that I'm almost naked.

When you get close to my doppelgänger, she might look a little thick skinned or sweaty, so stay back if it bothers you! She might not have a "beauty mark" on her lower back, but I wouldn't either if I could help it. Maybe the wax me could take over when the flesh me can't do it anymore. But the wax me would have to do whatever necessary thing it was in that fucking bikini.

Everyone else got to wear their regular outfits from the first movie. I had to wear my outfit that Jabba picked out for me. Jabba the Hutt—the fashionista. Jabba the Hutt—the Coco Chanel of intergalactic style. Trendsetter, fashion maven, leader of women's looks in his world, on his planet and the next. In wax, I would forever be outfitted by outlaw Jabba. In wax and out, I would forever be stone-faced.

I've rarely talked about Leia at length—not deliberately in any event. I'm asked about her all the time. How she is. What her plans are for *Episodes VIII* and *IX*. How things are going with Harrison. Is he feeling better since the crash of his starfighter—or whatever sort of plane/spaceship he was flying that day he crashed? Why wasn't I with him? I'll bet I was glad now that I'd stayed home. I wasn't going to let him fly for a while now, was I? That must've been scary, but then he always has been reckless, hasn't he? That's why you make such a good couple; you're one of the few people who don't take too much of his guff.

It turns out that it/she matters to me. Leia. Unfortunately. Sometimes I feel as if I'd rather concern myself with . . . almost anything. But as it happens I've spent the lion's share of my life, starting at nineteen and continuing forty years on jauntily in the present, being as much myself as Princess Leia. Answering questions about her, defending her, fed up with being mistaken for her, overshadowed by her, struggling with my resentment of her, making her my own, finding myself, keeping company with her, loving her . . . wishing she'd finally just go away and leave me to be myself alone, but then wondering who I'd be without her, finding out how proud I am of her, making sure I'm careful to not do anything that might reflect badly on her or that she might disapprove of, feeling honored to be her representative here on earth, her caretaker, doing my best to represent her, trying to understand how she might feel, doing what I can to be worthy of the gig, and then feeling beyond ridiculous and wishing that it would just fade away, leaving me to be who I was all those years ago.

Whoever that might've been before Leia eclipsed me, informed me, and made me angry and resent it when other people would try to put words in her mouth without consulting me! You mean I got to decide all things Leia only between sequels? When the camera goes on—I get handed a script to memorize?

What would I be if I weren't Princess Leia? A great big nothing without one piece of fan mail to call my own? Someone who didn't have to defend her right to not look good in a bikini over forty-five? With no bad hair to look back on wistfully? No nights spent thrashing around in bed sleeplessly wishing I hadn't used that awful Dick Van Dyke British accent while conversing intensely with a man in a mask who would turn out to be my father even though he'd used some horrible bad dentist in a sphere, giving me a root canal without Novocain as a form of torture? If he knew he was my father, why would he do such a thing? *Unless* it was to show me how good my actual real-life father was! If so, what an amazing (though delivered in an arguably life-threatening manner) perspective to provide me with!

Unfortunately, this perspective was delivered too late in my life to do me any real actual good. It could've been done to challenge me—force me, if you will—to *make* it do me good! It was done because he trusted that I had sufficient strength to be able to apply this insight! God never gives us more than we can handle, so if He gives you a lot, take it as a compliment—you catch the overall gist of my drift.

What would I be if I weren't Princess Leia? I would never give a celebrity lap dance or be considered a serious actress or have used the term "nerf herder" as though I understood it, though I didn't at all, never have met Alec Guinness or been a hologram where I recited earnestly a speech I'll remember all my life until I get dementia because I had to say it so many times, or shot a gun, or been shot, or not worn underwear because I was in space.

Never never never (I'm sobbing as I write this) have been

way overexposed. Or have had adolescent male fans think about me up to four times a day in a private place, never have had to lose huge quantities of weight, never have seen my face millions of feet high long past the time when that's a good idea, never have gotten a quarter of a point of the back end of the movie's gross.

Never have had the Force or a twin or been friends with a huge moody howling . . . not a monkey but . . . maybe a hairy creature. Never have been asked if I thought I'd been objectified by silently wearing a gold bikini, while seated on a giant laughing cruel slug, while everyone chatted gaily around me? Never have been in an airport and heard someone shout, "Princess!" as though that were my actual name, enabling and requiring me to turn around and politely respond, "Yes?" Never have had my entire planet blown up in front of me (including my mother and entire record collection), while looking at a small blackboard with a circle on it, never have talked to robots or teeny bearlike creatures whom I would then feed snacks. Never have been asked, "Who do you think you would've turned out to be if you weren't an intergalactic princess?"

I'd be me.

You know, Carrie.

Just me.

acknowledgments

For Paul Slansky there are no words. There are, however, a couple of facial expressions. Worry, which you abolished, and joyful relief, which you caused. No mere words—there are thousands of them, sentences and paragraphs filled with them. We row-row-rowed these words gently till I screamed—wearily, wearily, and finally cheerfully, this manuscript we redeemed. Whenever I get introspective, I frequently run into you.

For Billie—for turning out better than I could deserve or imagine. But please get a housekeeper. Vegas will always be there.

For my mother—for being too stubborn and thoughtful to die. I love you, but that whole emergency, almost dying thing, wasn't funny. Don't even THINK about doing it again in any form.

For Corby—for being the best assistant and travel companion I could have—working hours so long I couldn't see the end of them, helping me to make this the best book it could be. You beyond made up for those who went before you.

For David Rosenthal—for his assistance with the text, etc., and for the bum's rush in getting the whole thing done and out like fast food. Yes, you're good for the Jews.

Mr. and Mr. Stephen Fry, Beverly D'Angelo, Caren Sage, Ben Dey, Simon Green, Helen Fielding, Buck and Irene Henry, Clancy Imislund for the structure and patience; Dave Mirkin, Bill Reynolds, Melissa North Chassay and family, Gloria Crayton, Byron Lane, Donald Light for saving my mother's life and protecting her from demons and whores; Fred Crayton for keeping life exciting and being prompt in all things; Seamus Lyte, Fred Bimbler, Michael Gonzalez, Gayle Rich and brood, Gilbert Herrera, Bryan Lourd for his DNA, Paul Allen, Maritza Garcia, Roy Teeluck, Mr. and Mr. Rufus Wainwright, Connie Freiberg for finding all those early poems and knowing me my entire livelong life and not minding it; Mr. and Mrs. James Blunt and son, Blanca "Bubbles" McCoin for being such a good wife to what's-her-face; Graham Norton for keeping secrets-ish, J. D. Souther, Charlie Wessler, Griffin Dunne, Gavin de Becker, Bruce Cohen, Kathleen Kennedy, Dennis King, Sean Lennon, Cynthia, Martyn Giles, Cindy Sayre, Ruby Wax and family, Ben Stevens, Azar, Michael Rosenbaum, Art, Dr. Mike Gould, Edgar Phillips Senior and Junior, Annabelle Karouby, François Ravard, Kenny Baker, Katie Zaborsky, Timothy Hoffman, Penny Marshall, Michael Tolkin, Wendy Mogel,

Nicole Perez-Krueger, Carol Marshall, Peter Mayhew, May Quigley, Ed Begley Jr., Salman, Meddy, David Bathe, Johnny McKeown, Tony Daniels, NOT Bruce Wagner, Sheila Nevins, Fisher Stevens, Alexis Bloom, Nina Jacobsen, Joely and Tricia Fisha, Todd and Cat Fisher, J. J. Abrams for putting up with me twice, and Gary.

And
Melissa Mathison.
You are loved and missed.

photo credits

Leia, 1976.

Photo courtesy Lucasfilm Ltd. LLC. STAR WARS: Episode IV—A New Hope ™ *& © Lucasfilm Ltd. LLC.*

Between takes: Harrison Ford, Mark Hamill, and Carrie Fisher on the set of the first *Star Wars* film.

Photo courtesy Lucasfilm Ltd. LLC. STAR WARS: Episode IV—A New Hope ™ *& © Lucasfilm Ltd. LLC.*

photo credits

Carrie Fisher on Warren Beatty's shoulder during the filming of *Shampoo*.

Photo courtesy Getty Images/Bettmann

Carrie Fisher caught by a paparazzo outside Chasen's Restaurant in Beverly Hills.

Photo courtesy Getty Images/Ron Galella

Harrison Ford chats with Carrie Fisher during a break in the filming of the CBS-TV special *The Star Wars Holiday*.

Photo courtesy AP Photo/George Brich

photo credits

A promotion portrait for *Star Wars IV.*

Photo courtesy the author

Pages from Carrie's handwritten journals.

Photo courtesy Paul Mocey-Hanton

The princess, the smuggler, and a cast of thousands.

Photo courtesy Lucasfilm Ltd. LLC. STAR WARS: Episode IV—A New Hope ™ & © Lucasfilm Ltd. LLC.

photo credits

Mark Hamill, Carrie Fisher, and Harrison Ford getting a bite to eat on their initial publicity tour.

Photo Courtesy Getty Images/Steve Larson

Vintage *Star Wars* action figures released by Kenner Products.

Carrie Fisher, Gary Fisher, and wax Princess Leia at Madame Tussauds in London, May 2016.

Photo courtesy Ben Queenborough/ REX/Shutterstock

Photo courtesy Lucasfilm Ltd. LLC. STAR WARS: Episode IV—A New Hope ™ & © Lucasfilm Ltd. LLC.

about the author

Carrie Fisher is an author and actress best known for her role as Princess Leia in the *Star Wars* franchise. She has appeared in countless other films, including *Shampoo* and *When Harry Met Sally* and is the author of four bestselling novels: *Surrender the Pink*, *Delusions of Grandma*, *The Best Awful*, and *Postcards from the Edge*, as well as the memoirs *Shockaholic* and *Wishful Drinking*. Fisher lives in Los Angeles.

I have fill
unobtainable,
attractive an
company
Someone t
to enjoy. I
mercy. I s
lence, imag
ffering my
I am me
for not
I'm frighten
I feel I have

I was knee d
I couldn't let
Then just
When t
When
I met

In the past
It can all
At the
I see one of the
face
lling the shots
a first name basi
household word
able

all
he
ld
our
ate;
cious
the